The

Perfect Art of Navigation

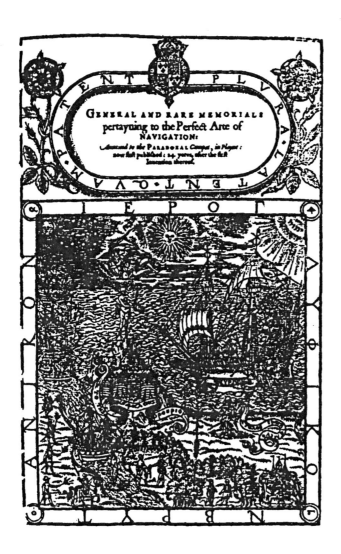

John Dee

GENERAL AND RARE MEMORIALS
pertayning to the Perfect Arte of
NAVIGATION:
Annexed to the PARADOXAL *Cumpas, in Playne* :
now first publifhed : 24. yeres, after the firſt
Inuention thereof.

A BRIEF NOTE SCHOLASTICAL, FOR THE better vnderſtanding of the *Decorum* obſerued, (or, at the *leaſt, regarded) in this preſent Two-fold Treatiſe, written vnder the Names* of Three diuers Proprieties, States, or Conditions of MAN: Wherby yt may appere, that they are not *Scopæ diſſolutæ*: or, *Du Coq à l'Aſne*: But, by the will, and Grace of the Higheſt, thus Recorded.

Firſt, yt was needfull, for the Vnknown Freend, *to declare his Senſible grief, conceaued, to ſee, and perceiue an honeſt Ientleman, and* Philoſopher, *by the malice and ignorance of ſundry his Cuntrymen, to be almoſt oppreſſed, vtterly defaced, and by dangerous reports, greeuouſly and dammageably diſcredited. And ſecondly, to make a mournfull, and dolefull Supplication generall, to all his Cuntrymen, to help the ſayd Ientleman to haue Iuſtice, and due amends, now at the end of his dayes. And all this, is the rather thus endited, that God his great Graces beſtowed on him, ſhould (to God his great glory) be acknowledged thankfully, and not be ſuffered any longer to be ſo craftily, wilfully, and violently trodden vnder foot, or barbarouſly deſpiſed. And it is likely, that, vnleaſt this* Vnknown Freend, *haue fauourable audience, and Credit, (in thoſe things, which in this* Aduertiſment *he declareth: being Senſible, both paſt, & preſent: pertayning to the forſayd Ientleman,) that the* Mechanicien *his induſtry, and great zeale, (vſed in collecting, and penning, from the ſayd* Philoſopher *his mouth, the* Hexameron *Plat Politicall*, of the Brytiſh Monarchie,) *ſhalbe but ſlenderly, and ſlightly regarded or wayed: and therby, the ſame to be found, finally, to les Commodity Publik, auailable. But, yf the ſame* Aduertiſement, *be earneſtly, ſpeedily, vnpartially, & charitably examined, and conſidered, good hope may ariſe, that* Omnia cooperabuntur ad Vtilitatem Salutemq́;

temq; Publicam procurandam , ac promouendam,
expeditiſsimè & potentiſsimè . *VVhich, God graunt,
Amen .

*The Epiſtle in Meter, (annexed in the end of this
Book,) was by the* Mechanicien *ſent, after that the
vnknown Freend had (at his own charges, and with
his careful Trauail concurrent,) put the foreſayd two
Treatiſes, in Print: & deliuered again into the hands
of the ſayd* Mechanicien, *the whole Impreſsion therof.
The diuers Intents and purpoſes of which Epiſtle,
are eaſily to be perceiued . Therfore, yf
to haue ſayd thus much , was
neceſſary, the ſame alſo
may ſuffice.*

A neceſſary Aduertiſement,

by an vnknown freend , giuen to the modeſt,
and godly Readers: who alſo carefully deſire
the proſperous State of the Common wealth,
of this BRYTISH KINGDOM, and
the Politicall SECVRITIE
thereof.

Amentable and irkeſome,
are theſe our drery dayes:
(my welbeloued Cuntri-
man) Seeing the conditi-
ons of to to many, are become ſuch, as, to be to to
curious of other ✴ Mens
dooings: As though, they
them ſelues, were ſuperha-
bundantly perfect: or dwelt in Security , of not beyng at any tyme, hereafter, either ſurueyed, or con-
trolled for their own.

Nay, ſeeing the ſubtilty and impudency of ✴ ſome,
is ſuch, that they can, and dare, cunningly and craftily, conuey to them ſelues (or, to whom they liſt)
the Title and Intereſt of the thanks and commendation, due to other Men: who are not of ſo braſen
viſages, as to practiſe ſuch ambitious fatches for them
ſelues, or to procure ſuch malitious Diſgraces, to o-
ther : But are ot that myldenes of Spirite, as, P A-
TIENTLY TO ATTEND THE END,
which ſhall reueale the VERITY : when, iuſt
gwerdon , ſhall to euery Man be diſtributed , accordingly.

And thirdly , Seeing, ſome are ſo doggedly violent, and vaynglorioully doting, that they can not

Δ. ij.   like,

1.

Veritas (Vt fer-
tur) Odium pa-
rit. Ast ſanum
vt ſit, apud
Veritatis Oſo-
res, i ipſi etiam
Omnipotenti
exoſa Deo.

* Cur quidem
Vides feſtucam
qua eſt in oculo
fratris tui, Tra-
bem autem, qua
eſt in oculo tuo,
non animad-
uertis? Math.7

2.

Legas & re-
legas librum
Quintum Po-
liticorum Ari-
ſtotelis.

3.

like , conſent , or well ſuffer any od Man , beſide them ſelues : or , otherwiſe , then by them ſelues , to receiue due Salary , either of Credit , Commendation , or liberall Conſideration : where , their word or working (directly or indirectly) may hinder the ſame .

4. Fourthly , how pitifull is the Caſe , that * diuers , of ſundry ſtates , haue , (of Late ,) become ſo ſhameles lyers , and to ſome priuate mens liues , (thereby) ſo dangerous , That , if Credit had bin giuen to them , (by other , than the light hedded ſort) of ſuch Murders and Treaſons , as (moſt diuell like) they haue imagined , and reported to be : and withall , (wholy , of their own helliſh myndes , without any ſpark or drop of Veritie ,) haue fathered the ſame vpon the very Innocent (yea , ſo much an Innocent , as for any ſuch thought , in his hart , at any tyme , embracing or foſtering) : It had bin greatly to haue bin douted that the mighty wrath of God , would not ſo long haue forborn the iuſt reuenge (of ſo haynous abhominacions) taking , vpon , aſwell ſuch wicked and principall Forgers , as on other the fickle fauourers , or careles ſufferers of the ſame , any whit to preuaile .

5. Seeing the Prince of Darkenes hath ſundry ſuch his Factors : And yet , one * other kinde , more wicked and abhominable , than the rehearſed ; which are ſuch , as not onely , they them ſelues , commit Diueliſh horrible facts , but alſo practiſe other very fraudulent feats : And all , to their priuate Lucre onely : Chiefly ayding and furniſhing vp their own ſhamefull Credit herein , with the * Cownterfeting

of

of other honeſt and learned Men their letters : as, written vnto them , in ſuch their vngodly and vn-lawfull affayres: Or, as falſly, reporting their Con-ferences had with them , to the behoof (ſay they) of ſuch , as are become their miſerable and Coſened Clients .

And Sixthly, how, (almoſt, without remedy,) hath **6.** the moſt wily Tyrant , and Inſatiable Bludſucker, layd the plat, for a wofull Tragedy contriuing : yf, the power and Iuſtice diuine , did not bridle his maliti-ous Rage, and Infernall fury ? How, hath he (I pray you) inſinuated his Credit with ſome, ſo far, and ſo long ſince : that diuers vntrue and Infamous Re-ports, by their Siniſter information , haue bin giuen vp to ſuch, as haue gathered Records, of thoſe Mens Acts , who dyed in the Cauſe of Veritie ? And ſo, the ſame hurtfull vntruthes , beyng (yet) the ra-ther Credited, by reaſon of the Dignity of the place, wherin they were enſtalled , haue ſeemed , both to the foreſayd Diueliſh Coſener, and alſo, to the Cre-dulous Coſen (yea, and to very many others,) to haue bin a certain kynde of warrant : To the one, without feare , to Counterfet letters, or Diſcourſes, anſwerable to the foreſayd fowle vntruthes, vnadui-ſedly Recorded . And to the other, without ſuſpi-tion , lightly to Credit any ſuch matter, reported . And, ſo , hath the Feend Infernall , moſt craftily, and vnduly , gotten the honeſt * Name and Fame, of one extraordinary Studious Iendeman , of this land, within his Clawes : that, diuers his mere Maliti-ous , and wilfull Enemies , do verily hope , that it is impoſſible , that this Iendeman , ſhall , with this

Engliſh

Englifh or Brytifh State, either (during his life) be counted a good Subiect, or a Commendable, (nay, fcarfe a Tolerable) * Chriftian: or, any his Acts or Trauailes, all ready paft: or, other his intended exploits, of great Importance, fhall be, in this Land, acceptable: or, of the people, of this kingdome, receyued: as, by the fauour, light, and Ayde of the Bleffed Trinitie vndertaken, inuented, Compaffed, and atchieued: but, rather, by wicked and vngodly Arte, to be framed: and, by the help of *Sathan*, or *Beelzebub*, to be finifhed: vnleaft, the wife, or the peculiarly chief Authorized, will vfe due, Carefull, and Charitable Difcretion, From henceforth, to repres, abolifh, and vtterly extinguifh this very Iniurious Report, (for thefe xx. yeres laft paft, and fomwhat longer,) Spred & Credited, all this Realm ouer: it is to wete, That the Forfaid Ientleman, is, or was, Not onely, a " *Coniurer*, or Caller of Diuels: but, " *A Great* doer therin: Yea, *The Great Coniurer*: & fo, (as fome would fay,) " *The Arche Coniurer*, of this whole kingdom.

Before, that the (mentioned) Diuelifh Cofening was vfed: this fklanderous vntruthe was recorded, publifhed, and Credited: But, by thefe new deuifed Cofening forgeries, the fame, may (with fome) feeme to be vndoutedly confirmed. Oh Lord, with how tickle and ftrong Snares, and with how wily Laberinthes, hath the moft enuious Traytor, to the honor of our God and Chrift, bewrapped and Daunted many a thoufand of fimple & honeft Mens fantazies: inducing them, to Credit this Infamous Report: To Credit it, (I fay) in refpect of the

hono-

" If you will Read his Digreffion Apologeticall, conteyned in his Mathematicall Preface, to the Englifh Euclide (Imprinted A°. 1570.) you may the better vnderftand this point of this brief Aduertifement.

Oh, A damnable fklaunder: vtterly vntrue, in the whole, & in euery worde and part therof: as (before the King of Kings) will appere at the dreadfull day.

honorable Seat, wherin, it was, (very vnaduisedly)
set downe . In dede , euen he : who, at the begin-
ning , *sayd, *Ascendam in Cælum, & similis ero Al-*   *Esaia. 14.
tißimo :* euen he , hath setled this intolerable sklander of the vertuous, among the glorious Renown of
the Righteous : to so great hurt , and dammage of
the Ientleman (who, to all other Men, is harmles)
as, neuer to him, by any one Mortall Man, the iust
Amends, can duly be made . I would to God , this
foresaid sklander, and other Disgracing Reports , to
to rashly , and euen then ⋆ recorded , when this
Courteous Ientleman was also a prisoner himself: (&
bedfellow, with one Maister Barthelet Greene) had
bin , in due tyme espyed : and vtterly cancelled, or
razed out of all Records, wherin they were vnduly,
and vnaduisedly (first) admitted .

    Nerer to pres this Matter in particular , *it is* nede-
les . But, by this , and such like foule ouersight of Man,
& Cruell despite of the hellish Enemy, it is come to
pas (among many other great Inconueniences) that,
wheras the said Studious Ientleman , hath at God his
most mercifull handes , receyued a great Talent of
knowledge and Sciences: (after his long , painfull,
and Costly Trauails , susteyned for the same:) and
both by God, being warned , and, of his owne disposition, desirous, not onely to enlarge and multiply
the same, but also to communicate to other: He fin-
deth himself, (now, at length), partly forced, somwhat to yelde to the wickednes of these tymes, (being not possible to sayl against the windes eye): And
partly demeth himself (in Gods Iudgement,) excu-
sable, not to bestow any more of his Talent & Care-

          Δ.iiij.   full

full Trauailes, vpon the Ingratefull and Thankles: Nay, vpon the skorners and Difdainers of fuch his faythfull enterprifes: vndertaken chiefly, for the Aduancement of the wonderfull Veritie Philofophicall: And alfo, for the State Publik of this Brytish Monarchie, to become florifhing, in Honor, Wealth, and Strength: as much, as any thing in him, mought haue bin therto, (by any means,) found feruifable.

Solomon in Ecclefiaftes cap.4. So, I turned me, and confidered all the violent wrong, that is done vnder the Sunne: and Behold, the teares of fuch as were oppreffed: and there was No Man to comfort them: Or, that would deliuer & defend them, from the violence of their Oppreffours.

But, who would haue *thought, that they, who are (in dede) of the honefter fort, and more charitable: yea, of the wifer, and (by Office) mightier (& fome of them, taken for his efpecial great freends) would, fo many yeres, haue bin fo *Careles, or flack, to Ayde, and procure the Innocent, to be *deliuered, from the greuous, and moft Iniurious fpoyle of his good Name and Fame: and all the inconueniences, depending theron ? Or, who would haue thought, that fo great, & fo vncharitable Vntruthes, fhould fo vndifcretely haue bin publifhed: by thofe Men efpecially, who, otherwife, in woord and life, were very modeft, and Circumfpect ?

The chief occafion of this Aduertifement giuing.

I thought it good, Therfore (my honeft freend and Cuntryman) to aduertife thee, of fome parte of the Caufe, of the ftrange maner, of this Treatife comming to thy fight, or reading: As, without the Name, of any certain Author therof: And, without the Name, of the zealous Artificer, who firft did follicite, and collect fuch matter (by *Dictata*, as it were) from this Ientleman. And Thirdly, without my own Name: into whofe hands, the fayd Artificer, hath deliuered all the matter, that he could get

of

of this Brytiſh Ientleman : to the Title of this booke, anſwerable : yea, and other rare Inſtructions, alſo.

For (vndowtedly) this BRYTISH PHILOSO- PHER, is not only diſcouraged to labor, or pen any more Treatiſes, or bookes, him ſelf, in ARTIFICI- ALL METHOD, for his vnkinde, vnthankful, diſ- dainfull, and sklanderous Cuntrymen, to vſe (nay abuſe:) but, alſo, is loth (and hath great reaſon, ſo to be) to haue his Name, any more, prefixed, or ſubſcribed, to any Treatiſes, paſſing from him, either by writing, or by ſpeech.

And, both theſe Inconueniences, are purpoſely committed : to auoyd, or, ſomwhat to preuent henſ- forward, the farther grief and offence, that might grow to him, and his true freends : to perceiue the former ſundry ſorts of Caterpillers, and great hinde- rers of the proſperous Eſtate, of any Common- Wealth, to knaw vpon the leaf, or flower, of his Commendable Fame : who, would take very quick- ly an Occaſion (by the forefronts of bookes, garni- ſhed with his BRYTISH NAME,) to fall to a freſh pang of enuious buſioſity, impudent arrogancy, and dogged malicious ſpeeches vſing and vttring againſt the Ientleman : who (vndoutedly) wiſheth euill to none. And (perhaps) though it were very good matter, that ſhould, by him, be contriued and writ- ten, and vnder his Name, be publiſhed : yet, they would (in peruſing it), either peruert their own Iudgements of it, through their vnquieted, and mere malicious fantazie, wilfully bent againſt him : or, rather, in dede, through their own great Igno- rance, would verify the Prouerb : *Scientia non ha-*

bet Fnimicum , niſi Fgnorantem : as , they did by his
Monas Hieroglyphica : * dedicated to the late Emperor
Maximilian : wherein , the Queene her moſt Excel-
lent Maieſty, can be a ſacred witnes (as I haue heard)
of the Strange and vndue ſpeeches , deuiſed of that
Hieroglyphicall writing :

  Or, if they liked the matter : then , they would ſay,
that ſuch a Treatiſe, (vnder his Name , publiſhed)
is not , or was not , of his owne compiling and or-
dring, as Author therof : but that, ſome other Man,
now liuing, or long ſince dead, was the only and firſt
Author, of ſuch a good Treatiſe . And, that maner
of malicious Iniury, hath bin very notably done vnto him, for theſe many yeres paſt , about his Booke
Intituled *Propædeumata Aphoriſtica* : and is, yet, ſcarſe
ceaſed in all corners (for, it is backbiting worke, and
ſeeketh Corners.) For, ſome men, (And they ſuch,
who ought to haue bin honeſt and diſcreet , as they
are, or were accounted learned) haue, very enuiouſ-
ly, fathered it, vpon the excellent *Gerardus Merca-
tor Rupelmundanus*, (yet liuing at *Duysburgh*,) as, to
be the only and true Author of thoſe *Aphoriſmes*.
But, afterward , when that was found a peuiſh fa-
ble : Then, vpon one *Urſo* (who liued many hundred
yeres ſince) was all the Commendation beſtowed,
for that *Aphoriſticall* worke contriuing . And then, a-
gayne , after that , vpon one *Alkabitius* : And at
length, with ſhame enough (but more will follow)
being driuen from theſe mere enuious , and ſpitefull
falſe deuiſes : yet (moſt obſtinately and impudently)
they ſtill auouch to diuers Ientlemen, and certaine
Noble Men , that ſome other, or (in effect) any

Man

A. 1564.

Man els, was the Author therof: rather, than they would honeftly acknowlege the Truthe, of only this Ientleman his peculiar Induftry, and no fmall skill, v-fed in the contriuing and framing of that * Booke : containing the chief Crop and Roote, of Ten yeres his firft Outlandifh & Homifh Studies and exercifes Philofophicall : as, partly in the preface therof, to the Reader, is fpecified : but more habundantly and purpofely, hath that point bin * proued and teftifi-ed to fome, who were (before) fowly infected, with the sklaunderous Opinion, that one *Vrfo*, was the Author of it, and not this honeft *Brytifh Ientleman* : as, at an other tyme, will be made more euident : When, a ful declaration, in more conuenient place, may be made, of the mere malicious, very rafh, and Brutifh Cenfure, of a certain Doctor, (yet liuing.) Who, lately, endeuored him felf, to perfwade fome right worfhipfull Ientlemen, that it were good, and behoofull for this Common Wealth, If the fayd Philofopher, were *Banifhed* this land, for euer. Bi-caufe, faid this Doctor (but moft vntruly : as is now very euident, to Thoufands of Men, of this Kingdom, and other) That, to no Man of this Realm, he did at any tyme, or yet doth, or will, communicate a-ny part, of his learned Talent, by word or writing : But is wholy addicted, to his priuate commodity on-ly auancing, by his own Studies and practifes very fecret. That Doctor, his name, fhall not, here, by me, be difclofed : for that, he hath (vpon honeft Repentance, for his fo iniurious & dammageable In-tent) receiued his * Sentence of free forgiuenes : in the prefence of worfhipfull witnes, yet aliue.

*A°. 1 5 5 8.
In Iuly.
Firft printed.

*A°. 1 5 7 4.
In Auguft.
At Mort-lack.

*A°. 1 5 7 5.
In March.
At Mort-lack.

.ij.   And

And when, likewise, the perfect declaration may more aptly be had, of the most Iudas like pranke, of an other Doctor : who (in the tyme of this Brytan Innocent his Captiuity : and somewhat, before the day of his enlarging , by *letters, sent to his keper, from the Right honorable Priuy Counsail , to K I N G P H I L I P and Q V E E N E M A R Y) did, very ernestly sollicite with the Lord Chauncelor, (with whom he could do very much) And with

the Bishop of London, (whom, also, he could half perswade) that it were requisite , and Iustice, that the sayd Brytan Captiue , were not set at liberty at all : but , should be forthwith committed to P E R P E T V A L P R I S O N : And that, vpon such respects, as he, most vnchristianlike and maliciously, had deuised : and very impudently , vpon his Credit with them (such as it was) would haue forced , to preuaile . But, God would not suffer the sayd Courteous Captiue , his great freendship and humanity , a few yeres before, vsed toward that Doctor (in *Paris*) so, to be requited , with worse, then Ingratitude. Besides , that the sayd Captiue , could neuer (nor yet can) be duly charged, with any word or deed, vttred or done , contrary to the performance of his duty toward his Soueraigne and the higher Powers.

And though I here omit many other great Iniuries , done vnto him , about the bereauing him , of

the

the true and due Title and Intereſt, in and to his own works, writings and Inuentions, in other places recorded (And among that ſort, omitting that foule Iniury, done to him by one *Ioannes Franciſcus Offhuyſius*, whoſe booke *De Diuina Aſtrorum facultate*, was of this Brytan Philoſopher, his Inuention, chiefly: As, may be made euident, both by the matter therin contayned, being compared to his *Propædeumata Aphoriſtica*: And alſo, by the ſaid *Franciſcus*

his daily familiar * Letters ſolliciting and requeſting thoſe & ſuch like *Hypotheſes Aſtrologicall*, at the ſaid Philoſopher his hands: he being, moreouer here conuerſant with, and depending vpon this our Brytan *Mathematicien*, aboue a whole yere.) Yet I muſt Note vnto you, euen here, that one of thoſe Iniuries, was aboue all the reſt, ſo Notorious: and withall, ſo notably well * known, to be an Iniury, that the laſt yere, a certain Mechanicien, (being buſied about matter of Nauigation), calling to his Remembrance the ſame Iniury: being a fowle and Impudent * brag, that an Engliſh Mariner, (now, aboue, 20. yeres ſins) had made, to diuers honeſt men:(of the new Sea Inſtrument, newly alſo, called

* As may ſufficiently appeare by theſe few places taken out of ſome of his letters.

Doctiſſimo prob.eq̃, Indolis Dn°. Ioanni Deeo, ſuo Intimo.

Occupatiuncula me hactenus domi detinuere, &c. Quas de Aeris mutatione, concepiſti cauſas, ne relinquas, oro. &c.

*Ex Diuerſorio, raptim:
30. Octcb. 1553.*

*Tuus, ſi ſuus:
I-F van Offhuyſen.*

And agayne.

Suo chariſſimo Dn°. Ioanni Deeo.

Hiis proximis diebus, &c. Hypotheſibus ad Aſtrologiam confirmandam, quaſo, ſeriò Des (Vt capiſti) operam. Syderum ſedes, ſpero te Vtcunq̃, certas à me accepturum, ſaltem eorum qua per nos obſeruata fuere quandoq̃, &c.

Vale. 6. Nouemb. 1553.

Tuus Offhuyſius.

And agayne.

Domine, ſi non queas incommodè carere Ephemeridibus praſentis anni, obſecro, mitte: Et de tuis intelligamus ſtudijs. Ego diligenter planto ſydera. Spero, dum tua creuerint, quas concepiſti Hypotheſes, aliquid boni ſeminis nos collecturos. Vale fælix.

Tuus Offhuyſius.

* M. Steuen and M. William Borowgh, two of the chief Moſcouy Pilots (after the incomparable M. Richard Chancelor his death) can be ſufficient witneſſes, alſo:

* An Iniurious Brag.

.iij.   the

the *Paradoxall Cumpas* : As, to haue bin of his Inuention .) was so inflamed with Indignation against this
arrogant Mariner, his abhominable Impudency, (so
long tyme, by this Ientleman, very patiently suffred,)
that he made very earnest request to this Ientleman
(the true Inuentor, of this Instrument Paradoxal)that,
although, all the Iniuries receiued at their hands, who
were deemed learned , he would not very sharply
reproue : and, but at leysure: yet, that it should be
an Act, mete and needfull for him to do, (being also behoofull for the Common Wealth) speedily to
detect, such shameles Braggers and Crakers : onely
sophistically furnished , to outward shew : and that,
with other Mens rare Inuentions : but, of them selues,
vtterly vnhable to Inuent any worthy Conclusion,
to be profitably practised, on Sea or Land .

Which Mechanicien his ernest request , (by the
foresayd Ientleman) being graunted , was the very
chief & first occasion, of these Rare Memorials (con-

The volumes of Rare Memori-als, by what oc-casion they be-came to be writ-ten first.

cerning *The perfect Arte of Nauigation*) so comming
in Record : after a Mechanicall and vulgar Artificer
his blunt maner of penning, and collecting the same.
Who, about the Entrance into the matter of Na-

* The brief Ar-gument of the Preface, or first booke of the General & Rare Memorials.

uigation, finding good *Opportunity, to speake First
of a P E T Y N A V Y R O Y A L L , continually to be
mainteyned , for manifold great Commodities procuring to this B R Y T I S H M O N A R C H I E :(which,
no other way , can be brought to pas:) and among

Perpetuall Po-litik Securitie, is to be sought for: but not sluggish and rechles Se-curitie which is the ouerthrow of many a noble Kingdom .

them all, the P E R P E T V A L L P O L I T I K S E C V-
R I T I E and better preseruation of this famous Kingdom, from all Forrein danger, or Homish disorder,
to be the chiefest : and most needfull Publik Benefit :
(and

(and ·vndowtedly, likely, to enfue therof:)he was dutifully willing, rather to follow fome brief difcuffing
of that very waighty matter, (and efpecially in thefe ☿
dangerous dayes, and Incredible peeuifh practifes, ful
often deuifed againft the GOOD PEACE, AND
PROSPEROVS TRANQVILLITIE of this IN-
COMPARABLE ILANDISH MONARCHIE:)
then, to fall to the forefayd Generall and Rare Memorials recording, of THE PERFECT ARTE OF
NAVIGATION: which, he, (therupon) fet afide,
awhile. And wherof, now, only the Second Volume entreateth : vnder this proper Title : THE
BRYTISH COMPLEMENT, OF THE PER-
FECT ARTE OF NAVIGATION. For, no vul-
gar doctrine, or practife, is therin conteyned : But
rather the GENERALL COMPLEMENT, and (al-
moft in particular,) all that, which hitherto, was wanting : or, which mought be moft needfull to fo excellent an Arte, and (to this kingdome) moft beneficiall of all other Mechanicall exercifes:

And fuch is the forefayd Brytifh Complement,
(as I do right well know) that the Contents therof,
are aboue the moft part of the beft learned mens ex-
pectations, (yea, or hope) of being brought to pas:
and all that, in rare, general, and excellent Conclufi-
ons of Gubernautik, chiefly. And fo great, is the
Volume therof, that, to haue it fairely and diftinct-
ly printed, with all the Appertenances, it would be,
(in bulk) greater than the Englifh Bible, of the greateft volume: And yet, the plat of Inuention, Difpofition, and recording therof, was finifhed in les, than
4. monthes fpace: it is to wete, of September, Octo-

.iiij.   ber,

The Title and
brief Argument
of the Second
Volume.

ber, Nouember, and December laſt. Due Laud and Glory, be, therfore, aſcribed to the free geuer of all good and perfect Gifts.

The third Booke, I neither will, or may (as yet) ſay any thing of. The Ientleman his deſire was, that it ſhould be vtterly ſuppreſſed, or deliuered to Vulcan his Cuſtody.

But, the fourth Volume, I may Iudge it, to be as an Earthly Paradiſe : A Booke, of as great godly pleaſure, as worldly profit and delight : A Booke, for the BRYTISH HONOR and WEALTH (And that, in diuers maner) ſuch an one, as neuer, King *Ptolomæus*, or Prince *Abilfada Iſmaël*, or any Geographicall or Hydographicall Diſcouerer did write, or Collect: as I (for my ſimple Capacity) do verily Iudge of it. The Title wherof, is, OF FAMOVS, and RICH DISCOVERIES : The Diſcourſe therof, not only conteineth the Generall Suruey Hydrographicall, of all the whole world, (and chiefly the rare Euidences for all the partes therof, moſt Septentrionall) but alſo, a particular and ample examination, of King Solomon his Ophirian three yeres voyage: And alſo, the lawfull and very honorable Entitling of our moſt gratious and Soueraigne Lady, QVEENE ELIZABETH, (and ſo, this BRYTISH SCEPTRE ROYALL) to very large Forrein Dominions: ſuch, as in, and by the ſame, duly recouered and vſed, the Courſe of the Diuine prouidence generall, in this preſent Age, will bring to light and life, matter of great Importance and Conſequency, both to the Glory of God, and the benefit of all Chriſtendom, and Heathenes. The greatnes of this

Volume,

Volume, is not much les, than of the Second. And one way, it far paſſeth the Second : For, in the Se-cret Center therof, is more beſtowed, and ſtored vp, than I may, or (in this place) will expres .

The ſame Volume, was, chiefly, of the Iendeman his own very ſpeedy collecting : And (by his wil, and order) hath this Inſcription, or Dedication, To the most vvorthy : And the ſame Inſcription , to be written, or printed in letters of Gold.

And had not the Incredible, and manifold Iniuries, and vndue Diſturbances bin, which haue happened to him (by ſundry parcels of tyme) for the ſpace of three Monthes, and more, (in Totall ſumme), within the tyme of all theſe Collections , moſt ſpeedily and Carefully heaping vp togither , ſince Auguſt laſt : I am right well aſſured , that, neuer, in ſo ſmall tyme, ſo much matter, of ſo great Importance, with ſuch ſyncere and dutifull zeale to pleaſure his Natiue Cuntry : had by any Subiect (Brytish or English) bin de-liuered from him, by Inuention of his own , or by Circumſpect Collection , or diſcrete Application, out of former or preſent writers, and Authors.

What is than (I pray you) in all his life tyme, to be thought likely , or poſſible , and in tymes more commodious, to haue bin Inuented : Or, conuerted to better Method of Knowledge , or vſe of practiſe : or notably reformed, by the ſaid Iendeman? Eſpeci-ally , for the ſpace of theſe *Thirty yeres, laſt paſt? In which long tyme of his Tyrocinie , he hath , inceſ-ſantly , to the vttermoſt of his power , and hability, followed an extraordinary , and moſt painfull , and very coſtly Courſe of Philoſophicall Enquiries ma-king,

*In which ſpace of tyme he hath aduiſedly ſpent aboue Thirty Hundred pounds, for lear-ning of worthy Knowledges & Sciences: to the Honor of God aduancing, (far and nere,) and the better en-habling of him-ſelf to pleaſure his Natiue Cũ-try aboue all o-ther: howe little ſo-euer they haue (yet) deſ-ſerued it at his handes.

ⁱ.*j.

The Fruit, and end of Naturall Philosophy, boing vsed, as Christen men ought to vse it. king, after the best Verities: which, may yeld, (by due Considerations of the Creatures, their vertues and properties) to their Creator and ours, Glory, Praise, & Honor vnspeakable: for his Infinit Goodnes, Wisdom and Power: the euident print, & Demonstrable proof, wherof, the same, (our God), hath bestowed most abundantly, in his own handyworke, of all his Creatures Creating: all the whole, and vniuersall world ouer, disperséd: nay, rather Filling the whole Cosmographicall frame, and Orbe: from the Center therof, to the vttermost Circumference of the same : being, to Mortall mans outward eye, vtterly vnsensible.

It will appeare, hereafter, in due tyme, that, greater, furder, and of longer Continuance, hath bin his doings, and very well liked of, Aduertisements and Instructions, in sundry affayres Philosophicall, and Cosmopoliticall, FOR VERITIE, IVSTICE, AND PEACE FVRDERING, than hath, of any Three, of his neerest freends, and most familiarly acquainted Cuntrymen, bin (as yet) perceiued.

And this also, I may say of the same Ientleman (without seeming to flatter him, or any whit to abuse thee, my honest freend and Cuntryman:) or, he him self, with great Modesty, and no arrogancy, might (to God his high Glory) say: That, yf in the foresaid whole cours of his tyme, he had found a Constant & Assistant CHRISTIAN ALEXANDER: BRYTAN, should not haue bin, now, destitute of a CHRISTIAN ARISTOTLE.

Alexander.
Aristotle.

Any farder, is nedeles, to be disclosed of this Ientleman: whose greuous *wounds, (by dedly sklanders,

* The wordes of a sklanderer, are very wounds

ders,

ders, vpon diuelifh Enuy, only: and the fame, priuily flafht, and hewed into his Sydes: and nere vnto
his Hart) are not, yet, in the perfect and charitable
Chirurgiens, curing. The more Lamentable, will
the cafe be found: and the remedy, to late, thought
vpon, I am greatly afraid.

  In the mean fpace (my louing freend, and vnpartiall Reader) I am, to aduertife thee, that, as concerning the publifhing of the other two great Volumes: though, the Inuentions, and Collections be
fuch, as I fayd, and of great Value: both for the
Honor and Wealth of England, and
no little furderance of the Glory of God : yet,
(by Order, taken by him, who hath the chief Inte-
reft therin :) the fame, are not to be printed, vntil
the proof be past, How, this Mechanicien,
his zealous, dutyfull, and humble Aduertifement
Politicall, (for the Perpetuall Garde, and furder Seruice, of a Pety Navy Royall, to be maintei-
ned, without any Coft or Charge to the Queene
her moft excellent Maieftie, or any vnpleafant burden to the Commons, and faithfull Subiects, of this
Brytish Monarchie) fhall be liked of, and
accepted: (for the zeale, and matter, I mean, rather,
than for any Rhetoricall polifhing beftowed on it.)
Seeing, the fame, conteineth in it, fuch Fragments of
Inftructions, receiued from the forefaid Philofopher:
being, hitherto (almoft) a *Freendles freend. Why
fay I, *freendles? Seeing, a Ientleman, of great Experience in this world, fayd vnto him, in my he-
ring, within thefe few dayes:

    Tu certè Infœlix, at multos inter Amicos.

       ı.＊ij.   Wherby

and go through
vnto the inner-
moft partes of
the Body.
Prouerb. 18.

A Pety Na-
vy Royall
continually to
be mainteyned
without the
Queenes Maie-
fties Charges,
or any vnplea-
fant Burden to
the Commons.

* Exceptis,
Excipiendis :
ult illis qui-
dem paucifi-
mis.

Wherby, it might seme, that he hath many freends.
But, for all that, betwene a cold freend; and a faint
harted Enemy, is small diuersity. And vndowtedly, a
fayned, hollow harted or Hypocriticall freend, is
worse, ten tymes than an open Enemy: And, in very dede, is not to be counted a freend. And, so, may
the outward repugnancy of these two sayings, aptly
be reconciled.

  But, proceding in my former purpose, you may
vnderstand this, moreouer : that the Second Booke
or Volume, (to this Preface apperteyning) will be
of more hundred pounds, Charges, to be prepared
for the print (in respect of the Tables, and Figures
therto requisite): than you would easily beleue. Therfore, though there were no warning, of Attendance
to be giuen, to vnderstand the issue of liking or mis-
liking the foresaid, (zealously collected, and as humbly presented) Politicall Aduertisement : yet, this
matter of Charges, so far passeth my slender hability : and, withall, is so dreadfull to the Printers, for
feare of great los therby susteining (So rare, and few
mens Studies, are in such matters employed) that,
delay, on my part, is rather, that way, Constrained :
☞ And, therfore, no Order is to be thought vpon, by
*Till than, me, for the printing therof: *TYLL, A COMFOR-
TABLE AND SVFFICIENT OPPORTVNITY
OF SVPPLY, DOTH VERY VVELL SERVE
THERTO.

  And before, I bid thee Farewell (my Cuntryman)
I may yet aduertise thee, of one point more (whither
the sayd Second Volume, be euer printed, or no)
That, therin, is one parcell conteined : so, contriued

and

and Dedicated vnto the Æternall, Royall, and Heroicall Honor, and Renowm of our Incomparable Gracious Qveene Elizabeth: that, all the whole world ouer, yea, among the Heathen, as well as Christen: what language so euer they speake, that haue to deale with Hydrography, or Dangerous and long voyages by Sea: euen they, will, most thankfully, and for euer, sing and extoll her marueilous Princely Benefit herein: as, to them, chiefly for her Maiesties sake and Merits, imparted: who, hath bin so constantly fauorable, and so gracious a Soueraign Lady, vnto the Inuentor therof, her most faythfull and obedient Subiect. The richest *Pyramis* at *Memphis*, did neuer so far, and so durably spred the Fame and Commendation of the Builders therof, as these Tables Gvbernavtike, will win, and procure the large loue, and good liking of our Elizabeth, all the world ouer, and while the world endureth, to florish. The English Title therof, is, The Brytish Qveene Elizabeth, Her Tables Gvbernavtik. And the same, is of many Quires of Paper, conteining.

Now, haue I sufficiently (for this place & tyme) giuen vnto you (my courteous Cuntryman) Aduertisements: which (I trust) you will take in good part & thankfully: yf, in your own Conscience, you plainly perceiue, that all my zealous speech, herein bestowed, tendeth to the Aduancement of vertue, and to the great Benefit and Commodity Publik. At an other tyme, I hope to haue Comfort, and conuenient Opportunitie, to impart vnto you, other matter: for your exceeding good Contentation, and great delight also.

A strange Monument, Dedicated to the Æternall, and Heroical Renowm of our Queene her most Excellent Maiestie.

A Treasor incomparable for the Arte Gubernautik: and for very many other Experiences.

        ⸪ *iij.*   And

And, in the mean fpace, I truft that this my fyn-
cere, blunt, and fimple Aduife, fhall be fome Occafion, that henfforward, this honeft Ientleman, fhal
be fully reftored to the Integrity of his duly deferued
honeft * Name and Fame: And, alfo receyue great
Publik Thanks, Comfort & Ayde of the Whole Brytifh State. To the Honor, Welfare, and Preferuati-
on wherof (next vnto his duty doing vnto God) he
hath directed all the courfe of his manifold Studies,
great Trauailes, and incredible Coftes. As, both,
by thefe his *Hexameron Leßons* (Firft, here, for Security of the fame) fpedily Dictated: and alfo, by very many other his wordes, workes, and writings els:
both, in England, and other where, fpoken, done,
communicated, and publifhed, will, or may abundantly be teftified. And, fo, Fare you well in Chrift,
my Courteous, and vnpartiall Cuntryman: And, for
a Remembrance, at this our moft freendly Farewel,
take this heauenly Counfail with thee: *Omnia quæ-
cunq̃ volueritis vt faciant vobis homines, fic & vos fa-
cite illis: hæc enim eſt Lex & Prophetæ.*

Which kinde of skantlin, and Meafure diuine, being, before hand, and in due tyme, layd vnto all
our thoughts, wordes and dedes, may be as a good
and familiar Angell vnto vs: to help vs to fhonne,
and flie from all sklandrous fpeeches vfing: all malicious, or feditious Libels skattring: and all other vn-
iuft, & vncharitable dealings: yea, and from confen-
ting or fuffring of the fame, where we can, or ought,
to redres the Caufe.

And, Then, the Glory, and Peace of God, will florifh in this B R Y T A N M O N A R C H I E. Ouer which,

(fo

*Da operam
vt Fama tua
integra fit.
Hæc enim du-
rabilior quàm
Mille The-
fauri. Vita
quamvis bo-
na, ad breue
exiguumq̃, tē-
pus durat:
Bonum verò
Nomen, ad
perpetuitatem
ſtabile eſt.
Iefus Siraci-
da. cap. 41.*

Math. 7.

(ſo reformed) that our moſt Gracious and Soueraign
Qᴠᴇᴇɴᴇ Eʟɪᴢᴀʙᴇᴛʜ, may, very many yeres,
moſt proſperouſly and Triumphantly Raigne, it is
(vndowtedly) our bounden duty, feruently and full
oft, by Prayer, to requeſt at his hands, who is the
King of Kings, Almighty. To whoſe Protection, &
furderance alſo, moſt hartily, and dutifully, I com-
mende the very waighty Caſe, of this Common
VVealth: not vtterly vnduly, or, (yet) out of ſeaſon (I hope) in this firſt booke enſuing, ſomewhat
Conſidered of: as, in a *Preface, very nedefull, to
the Bʀʏᴛɪsʜ Cᴏᴍᴘʟᴇᴍᴇɴᴛ, Oғ Tʜᴇ
Pᴇʀғᴇᴄᴛ Aʀᴛᴇ Oғ Nᴀᴠɪɢᴀᴛɪᴏɴ.
And herewith, (once more), I ſay, *Adieu:*
and well moteſt thou Fare, my Chriſtian Brother, and ſyncerely be-
loued Cuntryman.

* The firſt Book here following, is but (as it were) a Pre-face: To the Second, contey-ning in it the Art, to this kingdome moſt beneficiall,if it might be duely vſed.

*Anno, Stellæ (Cælo Demiſſæ,
rectáq̕ Reuerſæ) Quinto:
Julij verò, Die. 4.*
ᴇᴛ
Anno Mundi,
5540.

TO THE RIGHT WOR-

shipfull, difcrete, and finguler fauorer, of all
good Artes, and Sciences, M. Chriftopher Hatton
Efquier : Capitain of her Maiefties Garde, and
Ientleman of her priuy Chamber.

Ot.onely my dutifull good will toward your
Worfhip, and my great defire, to doo fome
thing beneficiall to this my Natiue Cuntry: But
allfo, a certain ftinging Indignation, agaynft
the Impudent Attempt of fuch, as vfe, wrong-
fully to challendge to them felues, other mens
Trauailes, (and not hable to yeld any Ingenious Inuention of their own) haue, at this *prefent, forced me, to doo my Indeuor, for the
publifhing of this ftrange Inftrument, with the
name of the true Inuentor therof, annexed:
And humbly to dedicate my fimple Induftry herein, to your worfhips protection. Truftyng you will the rather accept the fame, beyng (as it were)
a Crum, to my great Contentation, faln from his plentifull Table, whom
(I am affured) you doo derely and fincerely, both loue and efteme: as
well, of your own moft curteous difpofition toward all men, with whom
your worfhip hath to doo: as alfo, for fundry his vertues, and excellent
Skill, in many Arts, and Sciences, Wherewith the higheft hath very
gracioufly bleffed him. For which his habilitie, and Talent, he is all
wayes moft humbly thankfull, to the onely Author, and giuer, of all
goodnes and wifedome. Verely, for thefe 24. yeres (at the leaft) I
haue had the Ientleman in great admiration: As well for his forefayd
excellencie in good learning (fo iudged of, long fins, by the learned, in
fundry Nations) As, for his moft ready Curtefie in Communicating or
conferring to and with fuch, as duly require his Aduife, Opinion, or
Iudgement, in any Science, Arte or Practife, wherein he hath had
any fpeculation or exercife. Such Commendations, as thefe, allthough
they be great, (and rare, in any Studious Ientleman of this Kingdom,
els:) Yet, neither the fame, nor ten tymes as great (fownding lowd
about his eares, for thefe many yeres paft) haue at any tyme, or yet
doo, any one pyns point, puf vp his hart, vaynglorioufly: but haue,
and doo make him more Ioyfully thankfull, to the kingly and free giuer,
of fuch his great Talent: So great, as, *Quibus Res nota funt, & qui illi
bene volunt, exiftimant orationem non effe parem Magnitudini Rerum gefta-
rum,* (As that prudent Athenienfien Gouernor, Pericles, fayd, In
oratione Funebri: Commending them, that manfully had fpent their
liues, in the late warres, then:) *Alij, ignari, iudicant laudes effe im-
modicas: quia inuident excellenti virtuti. Laudes enim eo vfq; tolerabiles funt,
donec ea dicuntur, qua Auditores fe quoq; facere poffe arbitrantur: Si Maiora
dicuntur,* Inuident, non credunt.

Therfore, pardon me (I befeech your worfhip) Yf in rehearfing
here, and there (glaunfingly) fome points of his due Commendation,

A.i.   I fpeak

*An. 1576
Augufti. 1.

Thucidides,
Lib. 2.

I fpeak far fhort of that, which (farder) your worfhip and other, doo, or may know and more aptly can expres, to Gods glory : for his graces, on that Ientleman, fo abundantly beftowed : Who (I know right well) doth make no les account of your Worfhip, then the Iuftice of dutifull and perfect Amitie requireth. Which is a thing, very rare(now a dayes) any where to be found. And for better proof of the Premiffes, (by your leaue, and with your patience) I will, here, truly and briefly Note fuch matter vnto you, as neither (Withall) is impertinent to this Para-doxall Inftrument, now, firft publifhed : nor mete to be let pas (in a manner) vnknown, and vtterly vnrecorded.

For, whereas, about, 3. or 4. monthes laft paft, a vertuous * Ientleman and Marchant, with zealous Intent, for the Auauncement of God his glory, and the great Commoditie, and honor of this kingdom, procured vnto him, Worfhipfull, yea and Honorable Ayde alfo : to fet furth Ships, for a Northweft Difcouery : And fhortly after, there came abrode, in Print, a little Englifh book, containing fome probable rea-fons, tending to the perfwafion of the fame Cours and voyage : In the Epiftle of which little book, no fmall pece of Credit (for the Attempt to be liked of) was afcribed to *M. Dee* his Iudgement, (as, there, is to be fene) fet down, in his Mathematicall Præface, with the En-glifh Euclide, publifhed : So it came to pas, that it was his wur-fhipfull freend (*M. Edward Dyer*) his fortune, Firft, to Aduertife him (as he told me) both of the fayd book, by the Title therof : and of his Name, in the forefayd Epiftle (to good purpofe) vfed. Whereupon, he, calling to Remembrance his old Atlanticall Difcourfes, to the felf fame purpofe (at the fayd *M. Dyer* his requeft) almoft ten yeres fins, fet down in writyng : And perufing throughly all reafons and allegations (both *Pro* and *Contra*) now, in the fayd Pamphlet expreffed : did, furth-with, by euery Article therof, in the Margent, Note their value, or imperfection. And, ftraight way, after that, made a new Collection, for the fame voyage, very probable. And thirdly (the fame day) writ, 18. new Confiderations of his own : very pleafant, in probabilitie, for an other voyage of Difcouery :(in refpect of Safetie, Nerenes, and Com-moditie) nothing inferior to that, which they, * now, haue vnderta-ken, God fend them good fpede.

And, M. Dee, being thus furnifhed, afwell to maintein proba-bly his former Iudgement (by *M. Gafcoyn* recited, in the forefayd Epi-ftle) and intending to geue thofe his, 18. new and very ftraunge Articles of Confideration, to him or them, whom he fhould deme apt and de-firous to furder the fayd Difcouery (no les, then this was by a difcrete, carefull, diligent, and conftant Procurer, follower and furderer, brought to the prefent execution) : And alfo, purpofing freendly to examin, and faithfully to Inftruct *M. Capitain Frobifher*, and *M. Chriftopher Hall*, and other, that fhould haue the chardge about the fayd Northweft Dif-couery (As he was, partly by the right worfhipfull Sir *Leonell Ducket* Knight, and partly by *M. Frobifher* him felf, before that, requefted to doo) made, then, no delay, to repayr to the Mofchouy houfe :

Where,

M.M. Lok.

* They did fet furth the 12. of Iune laft.

Where, he found him felf courteoufly and very worfhipfully enterteined. And at that tyme of his abode there, and after that, at fundry other tymes, of his Refort, thither, and to their Ships, he proceded fo with them, according to his Intent: and pleafured them, fo much according to their defire: That he finding them, quick of apprehenfion, and likely to remaine * Thankfull, for his pithy inftructing of them: And they, finding him (aboue their expectation) fkilfull: And (more then could be wifhed for) Carefull, for their well doing, in this their commendable and honorable Attempt: both the one and the other, became very forry of their fo late acquaintance and conference, for thefe their waighty affaires furdering: And greatly mifliked their want of tyme, fufficient for the *Complement and principall pointes of the Perfect Art of Nauigation* learning at his hands. Such pointes, (I meane), as needed either great knowledge in the *Sciences Mathematicall, and Arts Mechanicall:*

The Complement of the perfect Art of Nauigation.

As (befides many other thinges) this letter, may ferue to be a fufficient witnes.

To the worfhipfull and our approued good freend M. Dee, giue thefe with fpeed.

This 26. of Iune. 1576. I ariued in Shotland in the Bay of Saint Tronions in the Latitude of 59 degrees, 46 Minutes.

I with M. Hall make our dutifull Commendations to you with as many thankes as we can with...

Your louing frend to vfe and command Martin Frobifher.

Yours to command Chriftopher Hall.

or expert Skill, of many *Caufes and effects Naturall:* Such points (I fay) to their affaires, and the *Perfect Art of Nauigation*, incident: he very aptly could, & right willingly wold haue dealt with them in: Yf that pinch of tyme, wold haue fo permitted. For, it is very euident, by his defcription *of the Perfect Art of Nauigation* (in his forefayd *Mathematicall Preface*, declared) and alfo, common reafon, and dayly experience, will confirme the fame: that, not onely, fuch fkill and furniture, as both here is rehearfed, and in that Præface is fpecified: But, other alfo, is moft nedefull for him to be fraught withall, that fhall be allowed for an exact *Hydrographer, Pylot-Maior, Arche-Pylot, or Grand-Pylot-Generall* of fuch an Incomparable *Ilandifh Monarchy*, as, this BRYTISH IMPIRE hath bene: Yea, as it, yet, is: or, rather, as it may, & (of right) ought to be: As I haue bene informed by him, who can reafonably declare how:

THE BRYTISH MONARCHY.

WHom, alfo, I haue heard, often and moft hartily Wifh, That all manner of perfons paffing or frequenting any our Seas, appropriate: and many wayes, next enuironing *England*, *Freland*, and *Scotland*, might be, in conuenient & honorable fort (at all tymes,) at the Commandement and Order (by Beck or Check) of A PETY-NAVY-ROYAL, of Three fcore Tall Ships, (or more:) but in no cafe, fewer: and they, to be very well appoynted,

A very Commendable Wifh of a faythfull Subiect.

A PETY-NAVY-ROYAL.

A.ij.

ted, throughly manned, and ſufficiently vittailed.

The Publik Commodities wherof, enſuing: are, or would be, ſo great and many, as the whole Commons, and all the Subiects of this Noble Kingdome, would (for euer,) bles the day and houre, wherein, ſuch good and politik Order, was (in ſo good Time and Opportunitie) taken, and eſtabliſhed: And eſteme them, not onely moſt worthy and Royall Counſailers, but alſo Heroicall Magiſtrates, who haue had ſo fatherly Care for the Communaltie: and moſt wiſely, procured ſo *Generall Brytiſh Securitie*:

1. ¶ That, henceforward, neither *France, Denmark, Scotland, Spaine*, nor any other Cuntry, can haue ſuch liberty, for Inuaſion, or their mutuall Conſpiracies, or Ayds, any way, Tranſporting: to annoy the bleſſed State of our Tranquillitie: as, either they haue (in tymes paſt) had: Or els, may haue, whenſoeuer they will forget, or contemne, the Obſeruing of their ſworn, or pretended Amitie.

2. ¶ Beſides that, I report me to all Engliſh *Marchants*, (Sayd he) of how great value to them, and Conſequently, to the *Publik-Weale*, of this Kingdome, ſuch a *Securitie* were? Wherby, both outward, & homeward (continually) their Marchantlike Ships (many or few, great or ſmall) may, in our Seas, and ſomewhat farder, pas quietly vnpilled, vnſpoyled and vntaken, by Pyrates, or other, in time of Peace.

The wiſedom and purpoſe of that moſt politik Lawmaker, *King Minos*, may, herein, to vs, be a ſufficient Aduertiſement. For, * *Minos, antiquiſsimus eorum, de quibus audiuimus, Claſſem habuit. Et dominatus eſt in maxima parte eius Maris, quod nunc Hellenicum (.i. Græcum) vocatur: Et Regnauit in Cycladibus, & primus Conditor multarum vrbium in illis locis fuit, Cùm inde eiecciſſet Cares: & filios ſuos Gubernatores conſtituiſſet: Ac* Prædandi conſuetudinem *(ſicut conſentaneum eſt) quantum potuit, è mari ſuſtulit: Idque ob eam cauſam fecit, vt vectigalia & Redditus magis ad ſe peruenirent.*

What Abundance of Mony, now, loſt by Aſſurance, giuen, or taken, would by this meanes, alſo, be greatly out of danger?

¶ And Thirdly, how many men (before time of vrgent nede) wold, thus, be made very skilfull, in all the foreſayd Seas, and Sea Coaſts: in their Channels knowing, in Soundings all ouer, in good marks taking, for auoyding dangers, in good Harboroughs trying out, in good Landings aſſaying, In the order of Ebs and Fluds obſeruing, and all other points aduiſedly learning, which to the *Perfect Art of Nauigation*, are very neceſſary: Wherby, they may be the better hable to be diuided and diſtributed, in a greater Nauy, with charge of Maiſterſhip or Pylotage, in tyme of great nede?

For, this *Art of Nauigation*, requireth a great skill and induſtry. And, Yf, 2000 yeres ſince, it was found true, among the *Græcians*, that, *Ars eſt enim Res Nautica, ſi quid aliud: Nec diſcitur obiter: Sed ita exercenda eſt, vt in eam ſolam, cura intendatur, ne obiter ſimul alia agantur:* How much more, now, in our dayes, may it be truly affirmed: When, it is, ten tymes more, (in particular skill, and ingenious feats) augmented, then it was, in thoſe dayes? They of this Nauy, ſhould oftentymes eſpy or meete the Priuy Sownders and Serchers of our Channells,

Flats,

flats , banks , Pyts , &c . And fo , very diligently , deciphring our
Sea Coafts : Yea and in the Ryuer of Thames alfo : otherwhile,
vp to the Station of the Grand Nauy Royall . And likewife , very often , mete with the abhominable Theues , that fteale our Corne,
and vitrailes , from fundry our Coafts : to the great hinderance of the
Publik plenty of England . And thefe Theues , are, both Sub-
jects and forreyners : and very often , and to to euidently fene : and
generally murmured at : but , as yet , not redreffed : for all the good &
wife Order , by the moft honorable Senat of the Priuy Coun-
fayll , taken therein.

¶Fourthly , how many Thoufands , of Soldyers , (of all Degrees, **4.**
and apt ages of men) wold be , by this meanes , not only hardned , well
to broke all rage and difturbance of Sea , and endure healthfully all hard-
nes of lodging and dyet there , but alfo wold be well practifed , and eafily trayned vp , to great perfection of vnderftanding all maner of fight and
Seruice at Sea ? So that , in time of great nede , that expert and hardy Crue of fome Thoufands of Sea foldiers , wold be to this Realme
a Treafor incomparable . And, who knoweth not , what daunger it is,
in time of great nede , either to vfe all frefh water Soldyers : Or, to
be a fortnight in prouiding a little Company of *Omnigatharums* : taken vp,
on the fudden , to ferue at Sea? For, our ordinary Land mufters , are generally intended , or , now may be fpared , to be employed otherwife , if
nede be . I think , I haue fo hard , out of fome book , written *De Republica* .

¶How many Hundreds of lufty and handfome Men , wold be (this **5.**
way) well occupied : and haue needfull maintenance : Which , now , are
either Idle , or , want fuftenance : or , both : In to to many places , of this
renowmed Monarchy ?

¶Moreover , what a Cumfort and Sauegard , will it , or may **6.**
it be , to the whole Realme , To haue the great Aduantage of fo many warlike Ships , fo well manned and appointed (for all affayes) at
all houres , ready to affront ftraight way , fet on , and ouerthrow , any
fudden or priuy forreyn Trechery : by Sea (directly , or indirectly) attempted agaynft this Impire : in any Coaft or parte therof ? For,
fudden forrein Attempts (that is to fay , vnknowen or vnhard of to
vs , before their Readynes) can not be done , with great power : For,
great Nauies , moft commonly , are efpyed , or hard fomwhat of , and
that very certainly , while they are in preparing : though in the meane-
while (politikly) in diuers places , they diftribute their Ships , and their
preparations appertaining.

¶And , by reafon of the forefayd Pety Nauy Royall , Yt fhall, **7.**
at all tymes , not onely lye in our hands , greatly to difpleafe and pinch
the Pety forrein Offender , at Sea : but alfo (yf iuft occafion be geuen)

A.iij. on

on land , to doo very valiant Seruice : and that , ſpeedily : as well , a-
gainſt any of the foreſayd forreyn poſſible Offenders : As , alſo , againſt
ſuch of Ireland , Scotland , or England , who ſhall , or will trayte-
rouſly , rebelliouſly , or ſeditiouſly aſſemble in Troups , or Bands ,
within the Territories of Ireland , or England : while , greater Ar-
myes (on our behalf) ſhall be in preparing , againſt them : Yf , farder
nede , be . For , ſkilfull Sea Soldiers , are , alſo , on land , far more
traynable to all Martiall exployts executing : and therein to be more quick
eyed and nymble , at handſtrokes , or ſkaling : better to endure all hard-
nes , of Lodging, or dyet : and les to feare all daunger , nere or far : Than
the Land Soldyer , can be brought to the perfection of a Sea Soldyer.
As (to the ſame Intent) the Incomparable , and moſt expert Grẹke Capitain *Pericles* , in his Oration (had to the Parlement Senators of A-
thens) auowched : Comparing their State , to the State of the Lacede-
monians . Saying : *Cumq, Præſidium alicubi aduerſus nos collocabunt , nece-*

Thucidid.
Lib. 1.

bunt illi quidem : quia excurſionibus vaſtabunt Agros , & recipient Tranſſfugas :
Sed non poterunt ſimul & obſidere nos , & prohibere noſtras Nauigationes in ipſo-
rum terram : Vbs eos Claſſe vexabimus . At nos quidem plus habemus Induſtriæ,
ad prælia in terra , ex vſu rei Nautica : quàm ipſi habere poſſunt ad Rem Nauti-
cam , ex vſu Militiæ Terreſtris . Nec facile erunt periti Rei Naualis . Nam , nec
vos (quanquam à bello Perſico , Claſſe vtimur , & nos exercemus) ſatis Idonei eſtis.

8 .   ¶By this Nauy : alſo , all Pyrats , our own Cuntrymen (And they
to no ſmall number) wold be called , or conſtrayned to come home . And
then (vpon good Aſſurance taken of the reformable , and men of choice,
for their good Abearing , from hence forth) all ſuch to be beſtowed , here
and there , in the foreſayd Nauy . For , good accownt is to be made of
their bodyes , (allready hardned to the Seas) and chiefly , of their Courages and Skill , for good Seruice to be done at the Sea.

9 .   ¶Nynthly , Princes and Potentates , our forreyn frends , or pryuy foes,
(the one for loue , and the other , for feare) wold not ſuffer any Marchant,
or other , (Subiects of the Queenes Maieſty) , either to haue to ſpeedy
wrong , in their Cowrts : Or , by vnreaſonable delayes , or trifling Shifts,
to be made wery , and vnhable to follow their right : And , notwithſtanding
ſuch our frends , (or , Priuy foes) , their Subiects , wold be glad , (moſt
reuerently) to become Suters and Petitioners to the Royall State of this
Kingdom , for iuſt Redres : Yf , any kinde of way , they could truly
proue them ſelues , by any Subiect of this Realme , Iniuryed : and they,
wold neuer , be ſo Stowt , Rude , and diſhonorably Iniurious to the
Crown and Dignity of this moſt Sacred Monarchy , as , (in ſuch
Caſes) to be their own Iudges : or , to vſe againſt this Kingdom , and the
Royall chief Cownſaill therof , ſuch abhominable Terms of Diſhonor : as,
our to to great Lenity , and their to to barbarous Impudency , might
(in manner) Induce them to doo . And , all this , wold come to pas,
through the Royalty and Soueraynty of the Seas adiacent , or enuiron-

The Brytiſh
Impire.

ning this Monarchy of England , Ireland , and (by right) Scotland , and the Orknayes allſo , very Princely , prudently , and
valiantly

valiantly recouered : that is to say , by the sayd Pety Nauy Royall , duly and iustly Limited : Discretely possessed : and Tryumphantly enioyed.

¶Should not forreyn Fishermen (ouer boldly , now , and to to Iniurioufly , abusing our Rich Fishings , about England , Wales , and Ireland) by the presence , ouersight , power , and Industry of this Pety Nauy Royall , be made content , and Iudge them selues well apayd , to enioy (by our leaue)some great portion of Reuenue to enriche them selues , and their Cuntryes by : with Fishing , within the Seas , appertayning to our Ancient Bownds and Limits ? Where , now , (to our great Shame , and Reproche) , some of them ; doo come , (in maner) home to our doores : and , among them all , depriue vs , yerely , of many hundred thousand pownds : which , by our Fishermen , vsing the sayd Fishings , (as chief) , we might enioy : And , at length (by little and little) bring them , (Yf we wold deal so rigorously with them ,) to haue as little portion of our peculyer Commodity , (to our Ilandish Monarchy , by God and Nature , assigned)as , now , they force our Fishermen , to be contented with : And yerely (notwithstanding) doo , at their fishing , openly , and ragingly vse such words of reproche , toward our Prince and Realm , as , no true Subiects hart can quietly disgest : And , besides that , offer such shamefull wrongs to the good labourfom people of this Land , as is not (by any reason) to be born withall , or endured any longer : Destroying their Nets , Cutting their Cables , to the los of their Anchors : Yea , and oftentymes , of Barkes , Men , and all . And , of these forte of people they be , which (other whiles) by collour and pretence of comming about their feat of fishing , doo subtilly and secretly vse Sowndings , and Serchings , of our Channells , Deeps , Showles , Banks , or Bars , along the Sea Coasts , and in our Hauen Mowthes allso , and vp in our Creeks , sometymes in our Bayes , and sometimes in our Roads , &c. Taking good Marks , for auoyding of the dangers : And allso trying good Landings . And (so , making perfect Chartes of all our Coasts , rownd about England , and Ireland) are become (allmoft) perfecter in them , then the moft parte of our Maifters , Loadmen , or Pylots , are : to the dubble danger of mischief in tymes of War : And , allso to no little hazard of the State Royall : Yf (malitioufly bent) , they should purpose to land any puiffant Army , in tyme to come.

And , as Concerning those Fishings of England , Wales , and Ireland ; Of their places : Yerely seasons : the many hundreds of forrein Fisherboats , yerely resorting : the diuers fort of fish , there taken : with the appertenances : I know right well , that (long agoe) all such matter , concerning these Fishings , is declared vnto some of the higher powers of this kingdom , and made manifeft , by an other honeft Ientleman of the Middle Temple . Who , very discretely and faithfully hath dealt there in , and ftill trauaileth , (and by diuers other wayes alfo)to farder the Weale-Publik of England , so much as in him lyeth.

But , Note , (I pray you)this point very aduifedly : That , * As , By his plat , of our sayd fishing commodities , many a hundred thousand pounds of yerely Reuenue , might grow to the Crown of England , more than (now)

10.

R.H.

* 1. Note.

A.iiij.   doth:

doth : And much more, to the Commons of this Monarchy, alfo : befides the ineftimable benefit of plentifull vitayling, and relicuing, both
England : and Ireland : And befide the increafing of many thoufands of
expert, hard, and hardy Mariners : And befides the Abating the Sea
forces of our forrein Neighbours, and vnconftant freends : And (Con-
trarywife) the encreafing of our own power, and force at Sea : * So, it is
moft euident and certain, that *Principium* (in this Cafe) is, *Plus quàm
dimidium totius*. As I haue hard it verified (prouerbially) in many other
affairs.

   Wherfore, the very Entrance, and Beginning toward our
SEA-RIGHT Recouering, And the forefayd Commodities
enioying, at length : Yea, and the onely means, of our Continuance therewith : Can be no other, but by the dreadfull
prefence, and power, (with difcreet ouerfight, and due order)
of the fayd PETY-NAVY-ROYALL : being(whole fom
tymes, fometyme a parte therof) at all the chief places, of our
Fifhings : as yf they were Publik Officers, Commifsioners,
and Iufticiers : by the Supreme Authority Royall, of our moft
Renowmed QVEENE ELIZABETH, rightfully and
prudently therto afsigned.

   So, that, this Pety-Nauy-Royall, is thought to be the onely Mai-
fter Key, wherewith to open all Locks, that kepe out, or hinder, this
Incomparable Brytifh Impire, from enioying (by many means) fuch a
yerely Reuenue of Threafor, (both to the Supreme hed, and Subieds
therof,) as no plat of Ground, or Sea, in the whole world, els, (being of
no greater quantity) can with more Right, greater honor, with fo great
eafe, and fo little Chardges : So nere at hand, in fo fhort tyme, and in
fo little danger : any kynde of way, yeld the like, to either, King or o-
ther Potentate, and abfolute Gouernour therof, whofoeuer. Befides the
Peaceable Security, to enioy all the fame, for euer. Yea, yerely and
yerely, (by our wifdom and valianmes duly vfed) all manner of our
Commodities, to arife greater and greater : as well, in wealth and
ftrength, as of forrein loue and feare, where it is moft Requifite to be :
and alfo of Triumphant Fame, the whole world ouer, vndoutedly.
Alfo, this Pety-Nauy-Royall, will be the perfed means, of very many other, and exceeding great Commodities ; redownding to this Monarchy : which, our Fifhermen, with their * Fifherboats onely, can neuer be hable to Cumpas, or bring to pas : And thofe, being fuch, as are
more neceffary, to be cared for (Prefently) then wealth.

   Therfore, the Premiffes well wayed, aboue and before all other,
this Plat of a Pety-Nauy-Royall, will (by Gods grace) be fownd, the
playn and perfed A.B.C. moft neceffary for the Commons, and euery Subied, in his calling, to be carefully and diligently mufing vpon,
or exercifing him felf therin. Till, fhortly, they may be hable, in effed,
                                                              to read

to read before their eyes, the moſt ioyfull and pleaſant Brytiſh Hiſtories, (by that Alphabet onely, decyphred, and ſo brought to their vnderſtanding and knowledge) that euer, to this, or any kingdom in the whole world els, was known or perceiued.

¶Furdermore, How acceptable a thing, may this be, to the Raguſyes, Hulks, Caruailes, and other forrein rich Laden Ships, paſſing within, or by any the Sea Limits, of her Maieſties Royallty, euen there, to be, now, in moſt Security, where, onely, heretofore, they haue bene in moſt Ieopardy: as well, by the Rauin of the Pyrat, as the Rage of the Sea, diſtreſſing them: for lack of Succour, or good and ready Pilotage? What great frendſhip in hart, of forrein Prince and Subiect: And what liberall Preſents, and forrein Contributions, in hand, will duly follow therof, who can not imagin? **11.**

¶Moreouer, ſuch a Pety-Nauy-Royall, (ſayd he) wold be in ſuch ſtead: As though, " One were appointed, to Conſider and liſten, to the dooings of Ireland: " And, an other, to haue as good an eye, and ready hand, for Scotiſh dealings: " An other, to Intercept or vnderſtand, all priuy Conſpiracies (by Sea to be communicated)and priuy Aydes of Men, Munition, or Mony, (by Sea to be tranſported,)& to the endamaging of this kingdom, any way, intended: 4 An other, againſt all ſudden forrein Attempts: ⁵ An other, to ouerſee the forrein Fiſhermen: ⁶ An other, againſt all Pyrats haunting our Seas: And therewith, as well to waft and garde our own Marchants Fletes, as they ſhall pas, and repas, betwene this Realm, and whereſoeuer els they may beſt be planted, for their ordinary Marts keping (yf England may not beſt ſerue that turne) And alſo, to defend, help, and direct many our forrein freends, who muſt needes pas by, or frequent any of thoſe Seas, whoſe principall Royallty, (vndoutedly) is to the Imperiall Crown of theſe Brytiſh Ilandes, appropriate. **12.** *The Marts*

One ſuch Nauy, (ſayd he) by Royall direction, excellently well manned, and to all purpoſes, aptly and plentifully furniſhed, and appointed: and *Now, in tyme of our *Peace, and quiet euery where (Yet,) before-hand, ſet forth, to the foreſayd Seas: with their Chardges and Commiſſions, (moſt ſecretly to be kept from all foes and forreiners) wold ſtand this Common wealth, in as great ſtead, as fowr tymes, ſo many Ships, wold, or could do, yf, vpon the ſudden, and all at once, we ſhould be forced, to deale, (for remouing the foreſayd ſundry principall manners of Annoyance:) we beyng, then, vtterly vnready thereto: And the Enemyes Attempt, requiring ſpeedy (and admitting no ſucceſſiue) defeating. *NOW. * Felix eſt ea Reſp. qua tempore Pacis, bella tractat. Laurentius Grimalius. fol. 71. Libro Secundo de Optimo Senatore, ad Sigiſmundum Poloniæ Regem.* **13.**

¶To Conclude herein · This Pety-Nauy-Royall, vndowtedly, will ſtand the Realm in better ſtead, then the enioying of fowr ſuch Forts or Townes, as Callys and Bulleyn onely, could do. For, this, will be as great ſtrength, and to as good purpoſe, in any Coaſt of England, Ireland, or Scotland, betwene vs and the Forrein foe, as euer Callys was, for that onely one place, that it is ſituated in. And will help to enioy The Royallty and Soueraintry of the Narrow Seas, throughout

and of other our Seas alfo, more feruifably, then Callys or Bulleyn euer
did: or could doo: yf all the Prouifoes hereto appertayning, be duly obfer-

ued: forafmuch as, we entend, now, Peace onely preferuing: and no
Inuafion of France, or any Enemy, on that Mayn, inhabiting: toward
whom, (by Callys, or Bulleyn,) we need to let-in our Land forces. &c.
Much (I know,) may be here fayd, *Pro, & Contra*, in this Cafe. But,
God hath fuffred fuch matters to fall fo out: and all to vs, for the beft, yf
it be fo (thankfully) conftrued, and duly confidered.

For, when all forrein Princes, our Neighbors: dowtfull freends, or
vndutifull People: (Subiects, or vaffals) to our Soueraign, fhall perceiue
☞ fuch a Pety Nauy Royall, houering purpofly, here and there, euer ready and hable to ouerthrow any their malitious and fubtile fecret Attempts,
intended againft the weale Publike of this moft Noble kingdom, in any
parte or Coaft thereof: Then, euery one of them, will, or may think,
that, (of purpofe) that Nauy was made out, onely to preuent them, and
none other: And for their deftruction, being bewrayed: as they wold
deme. So, that, no one, fuch forrein Enemy, wold aduenture, firft,
to breake out into any notable diforder, againft vs: Nor homifh Subiect,
or wauering vaffall (for like Refpects) durft, then, priuily mufter, to Re-
bellion: Or make harmfull Rodes, or dangerous Ryots, in any Englifh,
or Irifh Marches.

But, fuch matter as this, I iudge you haue, or mought haue hard of, ere
now, (by the worfhipfull *M. Dyer*,) and that, abundantly: Seeing, *Synopfis
Reipub. Brytanicæ*, was, at his Requeft (fix yeres paft) contriued: As,

by the Methodicall Author thereof, I vnderftand. Whofe Policy (here)
for the Partings, Meetings, Followings, Circuits, &c. of the Ships (to
the forefayd Pety Nauy Royall belonging) with the Alterations both of
Tymes, Places, and Number, &c. is very ftrange to here. So that, in
Totall Somme, of all the forefayd Confiderations, vnited in one: Yt feemeth to be (almoft) a Mathematicall demonftration, next vnder the Mercifull and Mighty Protection of God, for a fæfable Policy, to bring or
præferue this Victorious Brytifh Monarchy, in a marueilous Security: Whereupon, the Reuenue of the Crown of England, and
☞ Wealth-Publik, will wonderfully encreafe and florifh: And then, therupon, Sea forces (a new) to be encreafed, proportionally: &c. And fo,
the Fame, Renowm, Eftimation, and Loue, or Feare, of this Brytifh
Microcofmus, all the whole and Great world ouer, will fpeedily be fpred,
and furely be fetled. &c.

Truly, I was carryed (almoft, ere I was aware) and that, very pleafant-
ly, into the Confideration of the manifold and Incredible great Commodities, that may arife to this Kingdom, by A Nauy, fuch, as I haue (by
good Inftruction) fpoken of: whereas, my chief purpofe was, and is, to
entreat of matters, touching this Paradoxall Cumpas, and the perfect
Arte of Nauigation. But, feeing the word of a Nauy, was fo nere,
in Sownd, to Nauigation: And feeing, no Nauy (in dede) can be dealt
withall,

withall, at Seas, accordingly, without good skill of Nauigation : (though Nauigation, may be without a Nauy) verily, for so good a purpose, and so nere to my matter, I fauored my fantazy, while it somwhat strayed from my principall Intent. And not so, neither. For, my principall Intent and his chiefly, (whose brief Aduertisements herein I wold gladly make some Remembrance of) Is, (as it ought to be, of duty) to be sownd Euery Sublect his Duety. faithfull, seruisable, Comfortable, and profitable to the Politicall Body of this Brytish Common wealth : Wherof, we all, be Members, by God his mercifull Ordinance. That is to say : All true Sub-" iects, their Chief Intent, and principall purpose, (in all worldly their af-" fayres, Artes, Sciences, and Studyes, &c.) ought to be, the procuring, " furdering, mainteyning and encreasing of the weal and Commodity " Publik, so much as in them lyeth, and as, they decently and dutifully " may. And, So, the End of Ends, and yttermost scope of the sayd Arte " of Nauigation, is such Publik Commodity, of this whole kingdom " intended, and meant : that, from that Publik fowntain, very easily and " certainly, may be deriued to euery priuat man, his proportionall parte of delitious Refreshing, and vitall preseruation, in very godly sort, and politik order.

But, Contrarywise, Where priuate wealth and commodity is sought 1. for, before Publik : Or, no publik Commodity at all, cared for, or inten- 2. ded : but onely priuate : Or, where Publik Commodity and Security, 3. is euidently hindred, or, indammaged : There, by great wisdom, any such Common-Wealth, wold speedily be Cured from the Ruinous and Lamentable daunger, to the Strength and life of the Weale Publik ensuying, of those three kindes of so greuous and venemious wounds, if they be, ouerlong, neglected.

And, as Concerning the former Pety Nauy Royall : that I may, aswell Reporte some parte of his Plat, and Considerations, for the Charges thereof bearing and mainteyning, as I haue expressed his ear- The earneft wiſh of a duti-full Subiect nest wish for such a Nauy to be set forth, for the Causes alledged : After this manner, was his entrance into that parte of his discourse. What wold that Noble, Valiant, and Victorious Atheniensien P E R I - C L E S, say, yf, now, he were lyuing, and a Subiect of Authority, in this Brytish Kingdom ? What Common Contribution, wold his pithy Eloquence persuade, for the mayntenance of this Pety Nauy Royall ? Who, taught by word, and proued in effect, *Vnam Pecunia pa-randa rationem putandam, Naues quamplurimas habere : Alias verò extra eam rationes, nullius momenti existimandas.* And so, effectually persuaded the Atheniensiens, *Quòd, N A V E S, Diuitias : Diuitias verò, egestatem ducerent.* Which *Ænigma* of Prudent *Pericles,* is thus (in Latin) expounded out of the Greke *Suidas. Opes igitur in Terra, Inopiam arbitrari : In M A R I autem sitas esse Opes, existimare : Nihil aliud est, nisi vnas putare O-pes, Naues quam-plurimas : Reliqua, Inopiam indicare : Cuiusmodi est Pecu-*

nia

nia Spectaculorum, & Iudiciorum. Suadet itaq, Omnes in hæc factos sumptus, Nauibus esse assignandos. And, syns this matter of the Pety Nauy Royall, hath somwhat occupyed myne Imagination, I haue fownd (Sayd myne Instructor) by that worthy and excellent *Plutarch* his Grȩke histories, of Notable mens liues, that this *Peerles Pericles* (about two thousand yeres sins) faithfully and ernestly intending, to aduance the Atheniensien State, and Common Wealth: And to make it, after the best manner, to excell all other, with whom it had, or might haue to doo: perceiued, the only means, to be Such, as, by manifold, and more forcible Arguments, the like, must to this Brytish Ilandish Monarchy be much more auailable, To procure vnto it, Triumphant prosperity: And how? By Sea Security: And how, that? By this Pety Nauy Royall, in due * tyme prouided, and discretely, at Sea mainteyned. For, *Pericles* wisely vnderstanding, that no other means was so easy, so ready, and so sure, for Athens to atteyn to their wished for Souerainty, among their freends and foes, dwelling about them: But if, they were Lords and Maisters of the Seas, nere and far about them: he wold not lose any opportunity of fardering his purpose therein, both by Ships preparing, and apt men trayning vp to Sea discipline. And therupon wold not, *Imperitis Voluptatibus Ciuitatem delinire*: But with such exercises delight them, as, besides other their priuate Commodities growing thereby, The Principall and finall Publik purpose, might also therewith, be brought to greater nerenes. As: *Sexaginta autem Triremes quotannis emittere, in quibus multi ex Ciuibus nauigabant: stipendiumq, singulis octo * Minæ erat: qui eas pro meditatione, & exercitatione ad Nauticam & Marinam Disciplinam, perciperet.* This *Pericles*, also, by many his victories, was found and tryed, abrode (on Sea and land) *Vir bello fortis & strenuus*: as well, as, a most prouident and Circumspect Cownsailor, at home. *Nulla enim incidit (eo Duce) ne fortuita quidem Belli offensio.* And, *Quàm diù in Pace vrbi præfuit, moderatè vsus est Imperio, & tuta Ciuitas erat: Opibusq, ac Potentia (ipso Rempub: gubernante) præcipuè florebat:* As *Thucidides* witnesseth, and other. And now behold, what followeth (in *Plutarch*) noted, of some parte of that most comfortable frute enioying, which, of the former Ships prepared, And the Citizens to Sea discipline before hand trayned vp, was reasonably expected: *Deindè, Magna Classe, optiméq, ornata, & instructa, Græcas quidem Ciuitates, quarum ope & subsidio iuuabantur, benignè humanéq, tractauit: Vicinis autem Barbaris Nationibus, Regibus & Tyrannis, ostendit Potentiæ molem, licentiamq; & audaciam, quacunq; libitum foret Nauigantium: Maréq, totum, sub suam ditionem & Imperium redigentium.* O, a Sownd Cownsailor and Couragious Capitain, most mete for the Brytish Sea Royalty recouering. *O Pericles*, thy life (certainly) may be a pattern and Rule to the higher Magistrates (in very many points) most diligently, of them, to be imitated. But, albeit, that such a Græke *Pericles*, can not, readily, for our purpose, be found out: Yet, it is (Sayd myne Instructor) of some

Plutarch in Pericles life. Pericles florished An. Mundi, 3537. About which tyme, Plato was borne.

* Great wisedom it is, to vse OCCASION when it is present.

The marueilous Commodity, of being Lords & Maisters of the Sea.

* These eight Atticall Mines, were to be rated of our vsuall and currant mony, now. 25. pownds: very nere: and otherwise, to be named a hundred Crowns. For euery Mina Attica, was of an 100. drachmes. Wherof, 8. made the ounce &c.

of fome graue and expert men, thought probable, that this Politik De- An humble Aduertifement. uife, and humble Aduertifement, can not fo fone take effect, as all the States and the whole Commons of this Brytifh Impire, may, (for the manifold and waighty Refpects declared), both very faithfully defire, and alfo very quickly be induced, to be, after a moft eafy manner, Contri- butary thereunto : vnder the name of A perpetuall Beneuolence, for A PERPE- TVALL BENEVO- LENCE FOR SEA SECVRI- TY. Sea Security. For, who is there, of this Kingdom : A true and natu- rall borne Subiect (Spirituall or Temporall,) but very willingly wold : and without any his hinderance, could, yerely forbeare (to furder and ftablifh fo marueilous a Benefit publik)

> The Hundredth Peny of his Rents and Reuenues : and
> the Fiue hundredth peny, of his Goods valuation?

And after the fame rate, is to be vnderftode of all and euery Fraternitie, The peculier fpecifying, of the manner of Welth, you may confider in the Act, of the laft Subfidie, granted, Anno Eliz. 18. Guyld, Corporation, Mifterie, Brotherhood and Communaltie Corpo- rated or not Corporated, within this Realm of England, Wales, and o- ther the Queenes Maiefties Dominions, their goods and reuenues. And that, for onely the firft and immediatly next enfuing feuen yeres fpace. Then, for the fecond feuen yeres, to pay onely,

> The Hundred and fiftith peny, of his or their Rents
> and Reuenues, and the Seuen hundred and fiftith
> peny of his or their goods valuation, yerely.

And after 14. yeres expired, to pay for euer, but the half of the firft Contribution. So that, after the firft. 14. yeres fully expired, (after the day of this decree and Act making,) the Rate to be, yerely, but

> The Two hundredth peny of his or their Rents and
> Reuenues, and the Thoufandth peny of his or
> their Goods valuation, for euer,

The two Hun- dreth peny of Lands & Rents; And the Thou- fandth peny of goods (for e- uer) yerely, to be payable :

And that, I mean, onely, of all naturall born Subiects, of this our bleffed Iland ALBION. So that, fuch an exact valuation of their wealth and hability, fhould not hereafter (in any wife) be a thing to the Sub- iects and Commons, præiudiciall : And a caufe of greater Charge, or burden to them, in their Ceafments (to come) for any other Publik Ser- uice, or Commodity, than heretofore, the moft generall manner of fauou- rable * leuying, of fuch other Taxes and Subfidies, hath bene vfed : But, * As, one worthe 500.ll. in goods ; to be ceafed at 50.li. Beleue, vndoutedly, After that this SEA SECVRITY (with that fauour of the Omnipotent King, which he chiefly beareth to Iuftice and Peace : and by the wifdom, and pru- dency of the higher powers of this Impire) fhall be ones efta- blifhed, and confirmed, in trade of due execution, (either by meanshere expreffed, or better), Vndoutedly, * All other ex- * O, godly In- tent: O long looked for Có- mon wealth. traordinary TAXES, SVBSIDIES, RELIEVES, and LONES, &c. will ceafe, and vtterly be needles, FOR EVER. Prouided and excepted alwayes, that no man being A Promife. in the retinue of the Pety Nauy Royall, fhall with this Contribution be any thing charged : of what degree , or hability ſo euer he be . Suer-ly , Seeing God challengeth the Tenth yerely , and Firſt frutes , conti-nually : in Token of our Thankfulnes toward him , and for Mayntenance of the Leuites , that are of the Spirituall Miniſtery , Truly : the Tenth of the Tenth , I mean , the Hundredth parte of our Reuenues , As it is a les portion then the other , So will many thowſands , be more willing to geue it , and more truly to Recken it , alſo , then (now adayes) they doo the other : And will Iudge This new Beneuolence , as a gratious ,

* A Politik Eſter offring.

godly , & politik * Eaſter Offring , toward the Repayring and new Strength-ning of the ſowndation and Walls of *TEMPLVM PACIS* , or Solomons Temple , (as it were) I mean , of the whole Brytiſh Monarchie : Wherein , by this means , we may , in Peace , ioyfully , all the dayes of our life , and thankfully , ſerue the King of Kings , and Lord of Hoſtes : Little dreading , and les feeling the fury of any forreyn Enemies power . And thereby , alſo , be the better hable to cut of , and ſpeedily to

2. Repres any homiſh prowd fleſh , or Rebellious Carryen . And , as for the Free Denizon , yt is moſt reaſonable and fauourable handling , that he be Contributary herein , The Two hundredth parte of his Yerely Reue-

3. nues , and value in Subſtance : ioyntly eſteemed : And the mere For-reyner (here inhabiting) to be aunſwerable , yerely , for the Hundredth parte of his Subſtance onely . In their Natiue Cuntry , they know (and we are not ignorant) how far greater Sommes , they haue byn Tributa-ry of , yerely : and not , the Thouſand part , to their Commodity ſo auai-lable , as this will be : And as they alſo will gladly acknowledge : Yf they haue a faithfull hart : wiſhing (as they are bownd in Conſcience) the proſ-perous eſtate of this Renowmed Kingdom : Which , ſo charitably and fa-therly , in their neceſſityes , and half voluntary Baniſhments , hath re-ceyued them , and ſtill protecteth them : in no les Security , then the true and Naturall born Subiects of this Brytiſh Impire , are protected in : aſwell from all forrein violence , as all other Iniuries within this Land ,

4. ſuſtayning . Alſo , that euery Forreyner or Alien , (Denizon , or not ,) falling not vnder the generall reckning and order of Contribution afore-ſayd , and notwithſtanding , of the Age of ſeuen yeres , or aboue , ſhall yerely yeld to this Contribution , fowr pence , euery one , for a Pety Forreyn

5. Courteſy . Finally , of the wages of all hyred Seruants , the Hun-dredth Peny , of euery fiue Nobles wages , is to be accownted of , yerely : yf their meat and drink be alſo allowed them , beſides their wages : As moſt willingly , all Diſcrete Seruants , Engliſh and other , will yeld there-to . That is , of euery fiue Nobles wages clere , receyued , or to be re-ceiued , onely fowre pence to be due to this Contribution , yerely . And of any wages vnder fiue Nobles , nothing to be accownted herein , due. And aſwell , for the foreſayd forreyner , his or her Pety Curteſy : as alſo , for all Seruants , their fiue Noble Grote , of Contribution , The Maiſter , (or he , or She) , with whom the ſayd Forreyner or Seruant (or being both) is or ſhalbe abyding (at the tyme of Contribution , or Contributions ,) to be charged with the ſame , for lack of payment therof.

To be playn, and very brief: Who is there, in this whole Kingdom, so D
Temperate and Thrifty in his expenses: that dispendeth not, yerely, in very
vayn, and vtterly vnprofitable Charges, (I will not name some, worse,) the
Hundredth part of his yerely Reuenues: and the Fiue hundredth part of the
value of his Goods? Let euery man, vnparcially, examin him self, and his
own Case, therein. But, yf we, now, wold leaue of, such vanity, and (in
dede) folly, and turn that vayn folly to Ripe wisdom: And that superfluous
charge, priuate, to wealth publik : We may be iudged to haue geuen an
attentife eare, to the Kingly Prophet : and to haue bin obedient, to his
Counsayle : Where he sayeth : *Declina à malo, & fac Bonum: Inqui-
re PACEM, & persequere eam* . Syr, pardon me I pray you : for,
though I meddle not with the Mysticall and spirituall sense, hereof:(for,
I am neither Doctor, nor Bacheler of Diuinity : no, nor, of any calling
Leuiticall) Yet, truly, this exposition, or application, is not vtterly vnapt for this our purpose, of seeking wayes to preserue the Peace publik, with all forreyn Princes : And to establish the Security therof,
perpetually : So far, as humain policy, may make reasonable account, E
of so likely and circumspect meanes, duly executed,

It is an olde Prouerb. A Sword, maketh peace: So, this Na- *Herein con-*
uy, by his present readynes, and the Secret of his Circuits, and visitati- *sist sundry*
ons of sundry forreyn and homish Coasts, obserued : will make the mali- *Secrets.*
tious murmurers, and priuy malefactors, of all sortes, to kepe in, and
to forbeare their wicked deuises and policies : which, otherwise, against
vs, they wold aduenture to execute.

Moreouer, wheras, some are of Opinion, that prety Speede, were *Speede.*
nedefull, in the Premisses (as the tickle and perillous State of Christen-
dome, is, at this present :) Truly, in Respect therof, we haue great cause
to thank God, for the honest and prudent disposition of some Subiects of
this Realm : at whose hands (till Ships enough for the purpose, might
aduisedly be built) we may, partly buy, and partly hyre, both in number and goodnes, Ships, sufficient, to serue, in this Case, with all Opportunity .

But, as Concerning any of her Maiesties Principall Nauy, to be a- D
mong them, now, at the first, for Cowntenancing of their Credit,
or furnishing of their Strength, he wold not presume, to speake
therof : referring (very dutifully) such points, to the great
wisdomes of the highest Magistrats, to consider of.

And, Certaynly, if any thing, may (reasonably) be alledged, as a
Hinderance, whereby this Incomparable Ilandish Impire, shall be
barred (yet longer) from tasting of this most delitious, Comfortable,
Cordiall, and preseruatiue frute of * Peace and Tranquillity (politikly   1.
assured :) of * Wealth and Riches, comming in, abundantly, to Queene   2.
and Subiect: And, of right honorable *Renown, and great freendship,   3.
procured both nigh and far : Yf any thing (Sayd he) may seeme of Im- *Three great*
portance, that, probably and possibly may hinder this Publik Policy, *Dowts and*
from being put in execution : The first thing may be, a Certayn Dout, *Obiections.*
                          B.iiij.   which

which may ariſe among the graue Cownſaylers, and circumſpect Gardians of this Common wealth : Whether the Threaſor, by the former rate, generally in England leuyed and collected into their hands and order, will be ſufficient to counteruaile all Charges, ordinary and extraordinary, to ſuch a Pety Nauy Royall, appertayning, or no:

2. Alſo, they will, or may dout; whether vittailes will hereby wax ſcarſe, and dere, the whole Realm throughout, or no:

3. And Thirdly, the Poore and faithfull Commons, will on their part, only dout, of the true, due, and iuſt vſing and Beſtowing of the foreſayd yerely Beneuolence : and that, perpetually : according to the very godly and politik Intent of the perpetuall Contribution therof. Theſe three douts, chiefly, being reaſonably diſſolued, I will return to the Paradoxall Inſtrument, and other Nauigation matters, thus, a while, ſet aſide.

The Toucheſtone of all Subiects wiſdom.

This Nauy to be nothing chargeable to the Queenes Maieſtie.

As for the firſt : Yf the Toucheſtone of all Subiects wiſdom, that is, the Queene her moſt excellent Maieſtie, and her right honorable and faithfull priuy Counſaill, do like, this Pety Nauy (for the purpoſes before reherſed) to be ſet furth and mainteyned : So that, the ſame, become not chargeable to her highnes : but be ſufficiently prouided for, by the moſt eaſy and voluntary Contribution of her louing and faithfull Subiects, and other, (in maner, aboue ſpecified:) Then, it is to be ſayd to the Dout of want of Mony neceſſary : That, yf the foreſayd ordinary and vniuerſall Beneuolence of England, will not ſuffice (. Though it will amount,

1. Yerely, to aboue an Hundred Thouſand pounds) And eſpecially, ſeeing the greateſt Charges will be at the firſt preparations : yf all things be made and bought new : Yt is (vndoutedly) to be ſuppoſed, that many a Thouſand of Men and Women : Yea (in dede) the moſt parte of all the former Contributers, ſeeing or vnderſtanding the firſt yeres Contribution (before hand, deliuered) ſo well and duly beſtowed, toward their Intent performing, wold, preſently (vpon a Second Publik warning, of want,) of their own honeſt diſcretion, become (agayn) as Liberall and Beneficiall,

2. (and, but for this once) Extraordinarily, as onely the Six hundredth peny of their Goods and Reuenues, ioyntly, ſhould be of value. That is, for him that may diſpend, by Rents, of Lands, or otherwayes, a Hundred pounds, yerely : and be alſo, in Goods, worth 500. pounds, to yeld now, in extraordinary Contribution, xx. s. onely : and neuer, after that, any more extraordinary Ayde, to be, in this behalf, or otherwiſe, required.

Moreouer, in this Caſe of want, for ſuch a Publik Benefit furdering (as neuer was the like thereof, to this Brytiſh Monarchy ſo probably, aſſured) we wold craue, the Charitable and Brotherly Beneuolence (and that onely for this ones, As for the firſt ſetting vp, of the ſayd Pety Nauy Royall : And, but, according to this moſt eaſy, and Second

*Rate,

* Rate to be leuyed) of the Inhabitants of Ireland, Iernsey, Garnsey, the Counties of Northumberlãd, Cumberlãd, Weſtmerland; the Town of New-Caſtle vpon Tyne; the Biſhoprik of Durham : and of all thoſe Cities, Boroughs, and Townes (onely the Town of Barwick to be excepted herein) which by any Letters Patents, of the Queenes Maieſtie, or of her moſt Noble Progenitors, (otherwiſe) haue Exemption, Priuilege, & Immunities, from paying any Tax, or Subſidy. &c. And likewiſe, of the Inhabitants of the Fiue Ports, and euery of their Members : And alſo of the preſent Inhabitants within the Liberties, of Romney Marſh. And therupon, good and ſufficient *Prouiſo*, to be made, and eſtabliſhed, to all and euery of the foreſayd extraordinary Ayders; that this their diſcrete and voluntary Contribution, ſhall in no caſe (hereafter) be vnto them any thing præiudiciall, or dammageable to their Charter or Priuilege of Inmunitie.

¶ And this Requeſt, with no little Reaſon, may be offred to their Courteſies, to Conſider of : Seeing, not onely, it is for the better and more aſſured Peace and Tranquillitie enioying, ouer all theſe Kingdomes of England, and Ireland : and for a marueilous and Incredible wealth, and no les Strength, procuring to the ſame : But alſo, foraſmuch as, all the former, ordinarily exempted of all Taxes, and Subſidies, &c. ſhall, or may, by the continuall Seruice of this Nauy; and alſo by the Threaſory therof (hereafter) be greatly ayded : and that (peculiarly) to the leſſening both of their * Charges, and alſo of their * Danger, many wayes : In reſpect wherof, ſuch Priuileges, Immunities and Exemptions, were firſt granted vnto them : and continually haue bin, and are confirmed. So that, ſuch their extraordinary Beneuolence, ſhall not ſeeme merely giuen : no, nor ſo chargeable vnto them, as lent Good : But, to be Mony moſt commodiouſly (for their peculiar Cauſes, and behoof) ſomwhat before hand, diſburſed.

¶ Alſo, yf it were preſently known, that this Petty Nauy Royall, (vndoutedly) ſhould, for the foreſayd exceeding waighty Reſpects, very ſhortly, be conſydered of : And with conueniency and Opportunity, furdered to the ſetting furth, and vſe therof : vpon that True and ſufficiently warrented Aſſertion, and declaration : How many godly Aldermen, and other well diſpoſed Marchants, of the City of London : How many a Marchant Venturer, & owner : Yea, how many great Wooll Maiſters, Staplers, and Clothyers, throughout the whole Realm : Yea, and how many other, of all States and Profeſſions, wold very charitably, in their Legacies, Remember : or, be contented to be put in mynde, of deuout Contribution, or Legacy, toward the Threaſory augmenting, for due mayntenance of the foreſayd Petty Nauy Royall?

¶ How many a Biſhop, Dean, and Archdeacon, &c. With their own hands, wold (Extraordinarily) be example to the Layity, of turning, Liberally, the *Mammon* of Iniquitie, to the preſeruation of Publik Tranquillity : and the mayntenance of the Politik Security therof,

C.i. againſt

* Only the Six Hundredth Peny of Reuenues and Goods ioyntly.

A Prouiſo.

The Reaſon, why, of thoſe Exempted and Priuileged Places, an Extraordinary Ayde, is to be requeſted only this once.

4.

Legacies.

5.

againſt Fotreyn fraude and foĩce: and all Homiſh poſſible Rebellions ?

6.   ¶ But , and if the Incredible great, and manifold Commodities enſu-ing therof , were but had , a yere, two, or three , in proof : (O Lord) What lode wold be layd on , then , among the Godly , wiſe , and hable Subiects , to the better mayntenance of a bigger Nauy : And of new deuiſed , more warlik Ships ? How many wold contend with other , vertuouſly , to excell herein: as zealous Benefactors , to the Weale Pub-lik ? And ſo , for euer , to remayn recorded : not in boke onely , with pen and Ink marked : but in the harts of all Brytiſh , and Engliſh Poſteri-ty: and in their thankfull memories , deeply Imprinted.

Could the deuout zeale , and Intent of our forefathers , be ſo Bene-ficiall to Thouſands : And , without any Commaundement , or Requeſt Publik , (they being then , in darknes , and beclogged with Superſtition) moſt gladly , be ſo liberall , to the building of ſo many fayr Monaſteries , &c . Their decking, and Threaſory within: and enduing with Landes , a-brode (far and nere) to their charge , of ſo many Hundred Thouſand pownds , as , now , (in manner) are ineſtimable : And ſhall we , now , in the clere Sunne ſhyne of the pure Truthe and Goſpell: in the tyme of ☞ true Religion , known , and obſerued (As we will be cownted of,) Shall we , (I ſay) , be either ſo ignorant , how to vſe our Liberality : Or , ſo colde in Charity : or ſo blynde in foreſight : Or , ſo priuatly ſcraping , and miſerably hoording vp : or , ſo thankles and vnfreendly to the Common State of this kingdom : Where , both , our Anceſtors haue receyued their life , mayntenance and wealth : And we our ſelues , no les : and are moſt deſyrous , that our Childern , Wiues , freends , and Poſterity , ſhould enioy as great Commodities , by means of the Publik Society , and the Ciuill Communalty , being preſerued in Secure Tranquillity : Shall we (I pray you) in vertuous zeale , and Liberality , and chiefly , in theſe our Reſpects , of very needfull and certayn , very Godly and great Commodities enioying , be far Inferior to them , in their Reſpects , ſuch as they were ? We , being in wealth , and Reuenues alſo , far Richer , now : than they , then were ? God forbyd : that ſo great diſorder , and lack of diſcretion , ſhould be to be ſuſpected now , or to be douted of , in the people and Subiects , of this Godly , wiſe , and rich Kingdom.

¶ And How , can any Man , reaſonably doubt of the Hability of ſo mighty a kingdom , to ſet furth , and maynteyn moſt eaſily , only Three or Fowrſcore Tall and Warlik Ships : Where , ſo many Thowſand Thouſands , of folks , are Contrybuters to the Charges requiſite ? See-ing , only Forty or Fifty worthy Subiects , of their own pryuate Habi-lity , doo very eaſily , and (in manner) contynually , Maynteyn in trade , at Sea , ſo many (and more ,) ſuch tall Ships: And the ſame , well Ap-poynted , well vittayled , well Manned : and they , Duly payd:

The Pety Nauy Roy-all.   And chiefly , Seeing Such a Pety Nauy Royall , of Threeſcore Tall Ships , and eche of them , betwene eightſcore and two hundred , Tun of Burden : And Twenty other ſmaller Barks , (betwene 20, and 50, Tun ,) may be new made , very

ſtrong

ſtrong and Warlike : and all, well victtayled, for Six Thowſand, Six hundred, and Sixty Men : and thoſe Men , Liberally waged : And both Ships , and Men , to all needfull
purpoſes, ſufficiently appoynted : and ſo maynteyned continually , and that, very Royally , FOR EVER : for
les , then Two Hundred Thowſand Pownds Charges ,
YERELY , ſuſtayned.

The yeerely Charges of the Pety Nauy Royall , Will be les than 100000. Pownds Yereſly.

¶Moreouer , In Reſpect of farder by-help , toward the Charges
maintayning : Yt is not to be forgotten or neglected , that for a while,
at the firſt (and perchance, now and then, afterward) this Nauy, is
likely to mete with, and to Seaſe vpon ; Diuers Pyrats and Rouers: who,
either at broader Seas (you may ges , where) or els ; nerer hand ; haue
made Rauening hauock : And now , they, and their Goods , Threaſor,
Ships , and all , will fall into the hands, of Our Pety Nauy Royall,
or ſome parte therof.

Pyrats Goods.

Mary , herein, my Inſtructor , wiſheth ſome luſt and needfull Order to be prouided, and kept inuiolably . That ſuch Ships , Goods ,
Threaſor : &c, ſhould not raſhly , greedily , or diſorderly be dealt
withall . As though, we our ſelues , alſo , would be come Parteners
with Theeues : where , now , we are BY GOD AND OVR
GOOD QVEENE , conſtituted, as Diſcrete Iuſticers & faithfull Reformers of manifold Wrongs , at Sea , ſuſteyned :
And therin, to execute our Charge , aſmuch, and as conueniently, as
we may :

Therfore , after that ſuch a Pyrat , Ship , and goods , are vnder
our ſafe Cuſtody beſtowed : Proclamation : is ; ſo immediatly to be
made , that within a Monthe after , (or ſix weekes ſpace , at the far-
deſt ,) yt may be publiſhed in ſundry chief and moſt frequented Portes,
of this kingdom : lying , (as may vpon ſundry Circumſtances be gathered) moſt apt , and toward the places , either from whence thoſe
goods came : or toward which , they were to be caryed : with all ſuch
neceſſary Notice and Aduertiſement publiſhed , by the Proclamation a-
foreſayd , as may be auaylable to help the true Owners to their goods
agayne.

Prouing , good ſucces of , aduertiſements.

Thoſe taken Pyrats , alwayes , can (herein) beſt Inſtruct ,
where, of whom, when , and how , they came by that Booty : The
wares them ſelues , the Marchants Marks , Letters , Bills , Reconings
in that Ship or Ships , with thoſe Pyrats ſownd , will alſo geue ſome
light to ſuch Marchants here , as are beſt acquainted , with men of
thoſe quarters and Cuntryes , from whence , ſuch goods came : Or
whither they were to be brought . And, ſo, after the firſt Proclamation made , euery ſix weekes after , the Like to be made , in place conuenient , as before : Till a whole Yere and a Day ſpace , be
fully expyred , after the Day of the ſayd Pyrats taking.

And , yf , within that yere and a Day ſpace , No Claym be
made

A prouiſo.

made : That, then only , and not before , of All ſuch goods, (not yet Claymed), Sale be made , by Auction Publik. Prouided allwayes, that of wares , which wold , by ſuch length of tyme, take great hurt, or Periſh: (in good order of Auction,) Mony be made in due tyme. And then , owt of all manner of that Auction Mony, all Charges, vntill that tyme, ſuſtayned, to be firſt Diſcharged : And ſo, the whole Some therof, remayning : And the Threaſor alſo of Gold , Syluer , and ready Mony, (Yf there be any,) is to be diſtributed , after this manner, (* Yf it ſhall by the Higher Powers , be ſo liked of :)

*Yf, is here vſed, for that the whole doth belong to the Prince, by prerogatiue: and therfore it is here half Petitionally , and ſo, Conditionally reckened vpon: As, by the Queenes Royall bountyfullnes, which is alwayes to be hoped vpon, *in Rebus Reip Brytanica neceſſarijs:* And the rather herein, Seing none of her Maieſties Ordinary , ſtanding, or certayn reuenue is hereby diminiſhed : nor her highnes at any charges about the getting of theſe Pyrats: and ſeing her Graces Cuſtomes are the more encreaſed, when her Seas are free and ſafe from Pyrats.

* *In hoc , multa pereunt Reſpublica : Cùm qui Bonus & Strennuus eſt Vir, nihil plus quam Ignauus fert Pramij. Iacobus Simanc. Lib. 9. De Rep. Cap. 10.*

Diuide the Some, and Value of all, into Ten equall Partes. Wherof 4. are to be allotted to the Threaſory of the Exchecquer Royall of our Souerayn : 3. to the Threaſory of the Pety Nauy Royall : 2. to be ſhared among the Capitaynes, Souldyers , and Mariners : That is to ſay , among all the Men of thoſe Ships, which did preſent an actuall ſeruice, in the taking and Maiſtering of the foreſayd Pyrat, or Pyrats : and one parte of thoſe Ten , to be Due to the Lord Admirall of England, for the tyme being.

And as concerning the Shares, which are to be parted among the ſayd Seruitors of the Pety Nauy Royall : This , is Iuſtice : That (generally) it be diſtributed , according to the proportions of their Monthes wages : one compared to the other. And (particularly,) O d * Rewarde, owt of the Nauies Threaſor , is to be cheerfully and thankfully geuen , to whoſoeuer (at that tyme,) did moſt valiant and manfull ſeruice . And ſo, for a Second , Third , and Fowrth. &c . Yf it ſo fall owt.

¶ And of all Goods, Threaſor, Mony, and Iuells &c. By meanes of the foreſayd Proclamations (or otherwiſe.) Duly challenged : After all former charges, for the preſeruing therof hitherto, ſhall be accordingly payd, by the Lawfull Challendger: And vpon his paying alſo, only * the Tenth of the cleare value, of the ſo challenged Goods (the ſayd charges Deducted) Reſtitution, preſently, is to be made to the ſayd Challenger: And then, that Tenth , is to be diſtributed, in manner before expreſſed: by 4. 3. 2. 1. Yf the ſame be ſo liked of, By our Souerayn.

8.

The Tenth of Pyrats Spoyles, truly reſtored, to be contributed for a curteous recompence.

9 .

¶ To Conclude then : One other Chapter (yet more) hereunto, annexed , will make it moſt Certayn , that Threaſor will not faill vs , for the Royall and Triumphant maintenance ; of this our Pety Nauy Royall , And , that is : Yf yt wold pleaſe the Queene her moſt gracious goodnes ; to be ſo bountifull to the Commons , as to Geue , Graunt, and Aſſure FOR EVER, to the Threaſory of the foreſayd Pety Nauy Royall, all that her Right, Title, and Intereſt to the TENTH of all Forreyn Fiſhings, within the Royall Limits and Iuriſdiction of her BRYTISH SEAS of England and Ireland : where, now , No man, in her highnes behalf , or to her vſe, receiueth of any Forreyn Fiſherman , any one Peny, in token of their dutifull acknowleging her Royallty, within her due Limits of the foreſayd Seas .

A Supplication to the Queene her moſt excellent Maieſtie.

There

There is a dubble Title , and a Third Reafon, of this Lawfull de-
maund : The Titles , are thefe : Afwell for occupying thofe Our peculier Seas, and Sea Coafts, (to their great Gayn) otherwife,
then as a * Common Sea Paffage : And alfo, for that they fhall not
be , nor ought to be exempt of all Tything , there , toward God his
parte : where , with les coft , they receiue greater Benefit, then any Huf-
bandman , of Tylth of the Earth . In Refpeƈt (therfore) of Gods Glory : the Royall Authority , in our own Coafts , will Induce them , By
Right and Might , to Remember both God , and Queene, by whofe
fauours , they are fo greatly benefited , within our forfayd Sea Limits.

Which Limits (According to the Iudgement of myne Inftruƈtor,)
Are , in all places , to be accounted , direƈtly to the Myddle
Seas ouer , Betwene the Sea Shores , of her own Kingdom
(and of all Pety Iles , to the fayd Kingdom appertayning) and
the Oppofite Sea Shoares , of all Forrein Princes : And in all
Seas , lying immediatly betwene any two of her own Coafts
or Sea Shoares , the whole breadth of the Seas ouer (in fuch
places) is , by all Reafon and Iuftice, appropriat to her peculiar Iurifdiƈtion and S E A · R O Y A L L T Y .

The Proportion of the Equity of this Iudgement , dependeth fomwhat vpon the Ciuill Law , concerning Partition or Propriety of Iles
growing vp in frefh water Riuers . And it is not vnreafonable , to deme
Seas betwene diuers next Kingdoms, to be in like and Analogicall Condi-
cion , in refpeƈt of King and King : As frefh water Riuers , are , in Refpeƈt of Priuate Subieƈts , of one Kingdom, whofe Grownds are lying on
both fydes of the fayd Riuers : Though the Stream and waters therof (after a fort) be accownted Common .

Diuers priuate Groundes , haue , through them (by *Præfcription* fo
wonne , or otherwife purchafed :) Some, *Iter* : Some , *Aƈtum* : Some ,
Viam : Yet , no man , that , may there lawfully pas , may alfo lawfully
dig, to his gayn (or otherwife) *In Itinere* , *Aƈtu* , or *Via* , of that fort,
without furder and due licence obteyned. So , all high Wayes , are cownted Common and Publik, to pas in : But, for any Priuat Man, (though
he be a Subieƈt,) in any parte therof , to dig for a Quarry of Stone , or
myne for Owre , or Stonecoles &c . Yt is not lawfull : though he wold
fill it vp again, as well as he found it firft . So , here , the Brytifh Seas,
are Common , and free for all Ships of all Nations to pas in , and vpon:
But , as cócerning the Fifh , vnder the water of thofe Seas : (Which Fifh,
God & Nature, bringeth fauourably within the peculier Bownds & Iurifdic-
tió of Our Royall Precinƈt :) No Forrein Subieƈt, ought, cuftomably,
or otherwife (prefumptuoufly) therin , to caft Net for the fame : or , (v-
fually or prefumptuoufly) to ferch , or drag , to his priuate gayn , therin , without the efpeciall ʰ good leaue , of the Maiefty of our Souerayn
C.iiij.   Queene

The vfe of the Sea,
is Common, but
not the Iurifdiƈtion
of the Sea. And yet,
the fame, may be
Præfcribed : And
the Proprietie ther-
of fall to the Title
Royall Sƥd, Cepo-
lam Traƈlat. yde
Seru. Ryft. Cap. 26.
Fol. 95. columna. 2.
This is Bartolus opinion,
recorded by Cepola.
Habentes Iurifdiƈtio-
nem in Territorio Co-
berente Mari, dicun-
tur habere Iurifdiƈti-
onem etiam in Mari
Vicino , vfǣ, ad Cen-
tum milliaria : & pof-
funt ita Capere & pu-
nire Delinquentes in
Mari, vfǣ ad Cen-
tum milliaria, Sicut
in Terra, in quo terri-
torio. Quod Nota:
quia babui de faƈto
pro Venetis contra Ia-
nuenfes. Bart . Cepo-
la. Traƈlatu Ruft.
Prædiorum. Cap. 26.
Habentes Iurifdiƈtio-
nem in Terra, babent
etiam Iurifdiƈtionem,
in Mari & eius In-
fulis, valde remotis,
DVMMODO
alteri loco terreftri
non funt magis pro-
pinqnæ : Angelus, in
Lege , Infula Italia,
ff. de Iudicijs, &c.
Vide Cepolam Cap.
26. vbi de Confufio
in Mari ftatuendo,
æqve vt in Terra.
Which commeth
nere to the Æqui-
tie of this Philofo-
phicall Iudgment,
for the Determining
of the Royall Bry-
tifh Sea Limits.

Queene (the vndouted Lady and Miſtres, of the Sea Coaſts next adiacent) firſt obteyned : or, generally to be hoped for : *. Or, at the leaſt,
not expreſly known to the Contrary.

And herein, we deale, neither Iniurious̄ly or diſhonorably. For, we
will, to all our Oppoſite Neighbors, alſo attribute, allow, graunt and
yeld as good Right and Intereſt, for the other Moyty of the Seas, to their
Shore and Coaſts appropriat, as we do now challendge, for our peculyar
half. So, that, this is moſt Iuſt, Conſcionable, and Godly : Herein, To do, as we wold be done vnto. Which poynt, tendeth

Iuſtice, and good Conſci-ence.

greatly to the Aſſurance of all good Amity, and peaceable Traffique
contynuing, with our faithfull, or louing Neighbors.

And, Seeing Iuſtice, and God, is on our ſide, what Shame and diſ-
credit ys yt, or may it be, to vs, with all Chriſten Nations, (that ſhall
truly vnderſtand the Caſe :) yf we, like faynt harted and degenerated Mea-

NOW.

cocks, ſhould, now, make dainty, ſhrink, or be afrayd, valyantly to
ſeaſon on, and prudently to enioy, this ſo manifeſt Right and poſſeſſion of
our Sea Limits : and that, euery way ? being, in dede (where they are
greateſt) in reſpect of other Princes late Attempts, and Succes, of
enlarging and ſettling their new deuiſed Sea Limits : not ſo great a parte,
as a drop of water, is, in reſpect of a pottle.

Can that Pety Marchantlyke king of Portingall, haue any rea-

The Law : Quod Nulli-us in Bonis eſt, Occupan-ti conceditur.

ſonable Pretence : either, by Law of God, or Man, to inuade and poſſes:
not, *Quod nullius in Bonis erat, aut eſt* : But, many other mens Ancient
and lawfull Poſſeſſions, and Kingdoms : though they were, (and ſome yet
be) Infidels ? And that, in a courſe much longer, from his own, little,
rightfull, and originall Kingdom, than half the world is about, in the
greateſt Circle : yea, after the ſhorteſt Cut or Cours, which any way,
they can be brought, to the bounds of their late forced Royallty ? And
ſhall not we, haue the Courage and ſkill, rightfully to enioy the very
Precinct of our own Naturall Ilandiſh walls, and Royallty of
our Sea Limits, here, at home, and before our doores ?

Can the Portugale King (by the Popes Authority) cauſe the King of
Spayn, to make his Nauies and *Armados*, to forbeare comming within
any portion of the Eaſt half of the whole world ? (as, to enioy, or be maiſter of any Sea, Mayn, or Iland therein :) And alſo, will the King of
Spayn, be contented, ſo, to condeſcend and allow vnto the Portugale,
vpon condition, that the other half of all the world (Weſtward) mought
be at the like his choys and Iuriſdiction ? (And though, in dede, betwene
them two, and before God, this Couenaunt Negatiue, is firm, and inuiolably to be kept : Yet, neither of them, by any law, of God or Man,
can farder ſeaſon on, as their New poſſeſsions, but, as we, and o-

Note.

ther, lawfully, may : That is, where they finde, *Quod Nullius in Bonis
eſt*,) Can they, honorably (Quoth he) thus preſume, and with a Chri-
ſtien, Conſcience, Deale, Diuide and Share the whole world, betwene
them two only (*quo Iure, quâue Iniuria*) as much as they can : And will not
they, or muſt not they, and all our oppoſite Neighbours, be ſo rea-

ſonable,

fonable, yea and honorable with all; as to alow, like, and commend our wifdoms and Induftry, to enioy the fkyrts and Purlewes (as it were) of our Brytifh, naturall, and appropriat Sea Limits? And that, in the moft decent, peaceable, and freendly manner, that Princely Counfaylors harts can deuife, and moft difcrete Capitaynes; vnder them, can execute?

Well, (Sayd he) my Hope is, that vnder our good Soucrayn Elizabeth (ere long, if it be her pleafure) the Æquity of this Cafe, will, or may, be maryed, with the Security of the whole State of this Impire: And that they two, will bring furth COMMON " WEALTH, INVINCIBLE " STRENGTH; AND IMMORTALL TRIVMPHANT " FAME: Three moft lawfull Brytifh Childern; and long wifhed for, of the true, Brytifh, and Chriftian Druides, they being alfo, Politicall Philofophers, and not Sophifticate.

A Godly and Politicall Mariage, And the bleffed Offprings thereof.

Beleue *Pericles* his Saying, betymes: *Magnum eft, enim, potiri Mari. Confiderate enim, SI INSVLANI effemus, INEXPVGNABILES effemus.* Note, here, (I pray you,) a fowrfolde wife purpofe, vnder One golden Saying: to the Brytifh Monarchy (at this Inftant) moft aptly, applyable: *SI INSVLANI ESSEMVS.*

Thucid: Lib. 1. Pag. 93: SI INSVLANI ESSEMVS, INEXPVG: NABILES ESSEMVS.

Befides all this: Yt is moft erneftly and carefully to be confidered, that our Herring Fifhings, againft Yarmouth chiefly; haue not (fo Notably to our great Iniury and los, and the great and Incredible gayn of the Low Cuntries) bin traded, but from xxxvj. yeres agoe, hitherward. In which tyme, as they haue in wealth, and number of Boats, and Men, by little and little, increafed: and are now become very rich, ftrong, proud, and violent: So, in the Race of the felf fame tyme running, the Coafts of Norfolk, and Suffolk, next to thofe Fifhing places adiacent, are decayed in their Nauy: to the Number, of 140. Sayle, And they, from Threefcore, to a hundred Tun, and vpward: befides Crayets, and other. Wherupon, (Befides many other dammages, thereby; fufteyned publikly:) Thefe Coafts, are not * hable to trade Ifeland, as in tymes paft, they haue done: to no little los, yerely, to the wealth-Publik of this Kingdom.

NOTE.

But, the Herring Buffes, hither, yerely reforting; out of the Low Cuntries (vnder King Phillip his dominion) are, aboue. 500.

Befides, an Hundred, or fuch a thing, of Frenche-men.

The North Seas Fifhing, (within the Englifh Limits,) are yerely poffeffed of 300. or 400. Sayle of Flemyngs, fo accownted.

The Weftern Fifhings, of Hake, and Pylchard, are yerely poffeffed by a great Nauy of Frenchmen: who, yerely, do great Iniuries, to our poore Cuntrymen, her Maiefties faithfull Subiects.

Strangers alfo, enioy at their pleafure, the Herring Fifhing of Alamby, Wyrkington, and White Hauen, vpon the Coaft of Lancafhire.

And in Wales, about Dyfi, and Aberyfthwith., the plentifull

* Though of Lati in the Vlifhing & Low Cuntry Troublefome diforders, Some Few (by Stealling ouer of rittaylcs, and other things, from this Common Wealth) haue made them felues priuatly rich, and fo, Hable to fet forth, to Ifland, and to other places, a Ship or twoo: who (before,) were far vnhable therto, by their own Wealth, and Lawfull trade of Dealing.

Herring Fishing, is enioyed by · 300 · Sayle of Strangers.

But (In Ireland) Baltemore, is possessed yeerly, (from Iuly to Michelmas) most commonly , with 300 . Sayle of Spanyards : entring there , into the Fishing ; at a Streict , not so broad , as half the breadth of the Thames , against VVhite-Hall . Where, our late good King Edward (the Sixth,) his most honorable Priuy Counsaill , was of the mynde (once) to haue planted a strong Bulwark : for other waighty Respects , as well , as for his Maiesty to be Souerayn Lord of the Fishing of Myllwyn and Codd, there .

Blackrock, ys yerely fished by 300 , or, somtimes 400, Sayle of Spanyards , and Frenchemen . But , to Recken all , I should be to tedious to you , and make my hart to Ake , for sorrow . &c.

Yet, Surely , I think it necessary , to leaue to our Posterity ; some Remembrance of the places , where , our rich Fishings els , are, about Ireland : As at Kilsale , Cork , Carlingford , Saltesses , Dungarwen : Yowghall , Waterford , La foy , The Band , Calibeg . &c . And all , chiefly enioyed , as securely and freely , from vs , by Strangers , as yf they were within their own Kings peculiar Sea Limits: Nay , rather, as yf those Coasts, Seas, and Bayes, (&c.) were of their priuate and seuerall purchases : To our vnspeakable los , discredit , and discomfort : And to no small danger (farder) in these perillous tymes , of most subtle Trecheries , and fickle fidelity . *Dictum , Sapienti sat esto*

And , as for Ireland Fishings , some Towardnes of good Pollicy, and somwhat like reason of prouidence , was in the heds of the honorable Counsailors and Parlement Senators to King Edward the fowrth : When, in the fifth yere of his Raigne, this Act, (among sundry other ,) was established : That no Ship, or other vessell, of any forreyn Cuntry , shall go to Fishing in the Irish Cuntryes : And, for Custome to be payd, of the vessell that commeth from forreyn Landes to Fishing . Farder to vrge , or more particularly to specify the Conclusions, and reasonable Sequeles , as well of the words of the Act, as the Intent of the Act making, is needles, in this place.

Onely the
TENTH,
of Fish taken
by Forreyn
Fishermen,
within the
Brytish Sea
Limits, is to
be Leuied,
Discreatly.
Now , then , who can dout, (to begin withall) but that it is a most reasonable and freendly Request , of all these forreyn Fishermen , to require , (with all circumstances of humanity , Courtesy, and Freendship, therin , and thereto vsed,) The Tenth onely , of all their yeerly Fishings : by such means , as , most conueniently for them , and to our behoof, best, we may receiue the same : In Token , of their reasonable Acknowledging the ROYALTY of this Brytish Monarchy , in the selfsame Brytish Seas, and Coasts , to be , by God and Nature established: where , they receiue so great Commodity: and where, from hence forth , no Iniury by any Man of ours , shall be to them done , or offred : But , their thankfulnes to God , (in respect of Tithe) and their Freendly duty to the Royall Maiesty , and Imperiall Dignity of our

Souerayn

Souerayn Lady Elizabeth, (within her own Sea Limits) is , thus , in
rightfull , decent , and freendly manner , required.

¶ And here, alſo, the Third Reaſon of Demaunding the for-
ſayd Tenth (* before ſpoken of,) is to be playnly ſpecifyed : Which is * Supra Pag:
this . Wheras, the Herring Buſſes, and other Forreyn Fiſhermen; 21. Linea. 11
haue, heretofore, vſed to be at great Charges , with hyring Waſters
and certayn Ships (of their own Cuntry) appointed Warlike : for their
Garde and Defence, in the tyme of their Fiſhings , within our Brytiſh
Sea Limits.: Now (by the Politik order , and valiant Induſtrie of
her Maieſties Pety-Nauy-Royall , executed) No Pyrat, Rouer, or
Pilfrer, nor any Warryour, in Ship of War : No, nor Executioner of
any Letter of Mark , ſhalbe permitted to vſe; or haunt any of our Brytiſh Seas: and therfore, None of theſe ſorts, ſhall brede vnto the Forreyn
Fiſhermen, any Diſturbance , Los, or hyndrance, in the tyme of their
ſayd Fiſhings : And, beſides this; by the means of the ſayd Pety-Nauy-Royall, (contynually maynteyned at the forſayd Seas,) all manner of their Merchantlike Ships, at all tymes, may freely and ſafely
pas, and frequent; not only the Brytiſh Narrow Seas, but alſo Diuers other Seas: being within , or any thing nere the Walk and Circuits, of the ſame Pety-Nauy-Royall . Wherfore, In regard of
their ſayd great Charges * Sparing: And for ſuch Securitie * enioying * 1.
in the tyme of their Fiſhings , (Which two points , are by our Pety-Na- * 2.
uy-Royall, ſupplyed, and to them procured): And in regard of the
ineſtimable Los, and Dammage, aſſuredly preuenting, (againſt all Pyrats,
Warriers, and all other violence of Man,) Which, els , might happen
to their * Merchantlike , very rich Laden Ships ; Hulks, or other, * 3.
paſſing within, or nere the Circuits, which are (ordinarily and extraordinarily) of our Pety-Nauy-Royall , to be vſed and frequented ;
(Whereby, alſo, among their own Nation ; great Sommes of Mony, oftentymes, loſt by * Aſſurance taking; may, now, be ſaued.) In Regard
(I ſay) of theſe fowr, their great Benefits , by this Pety-Na- * 4.
uy-Royall, receyued : And in regard of the * Fyfth ineſtimable Benefit, and Riches, yeerly receyued , of the Fiſh : taken within our appropriat Sea Limits . And Sixthly , in reſpect of the Honor , Reuerence, Priuilege, and * Præeminence, which (By Law) is Due vnto
her Royall Maieſty, enioying the Lawfull Poſſeſſion of the Brytiſh
Sea Royalty (Though, for a few yeres, laſt paſſed ; yt hath byn by
Pyrats, and other, ſomwhat abuſed:) And * Seuenthly ; In reſpect of
Gods parte, and their Forrein Tythe , Duly and thankfully paying , of our
peculiar Commodities , by them receiued : And that, the rather: Bycauſe
her Maieſtie doth geue the ſame , For the preſeruation of So many, of
ſundry Nations, from the Rauyn of the Pyrat, and mayntenance of Godly Peace, and good Order; in her Royall Sea Circuits . And * Eighthly,
in Token of their Freendly, Honeſt , and Iuſt meaning toward vs ; And

in

Aduerte, quid
fuat tantum
4 Reges, qui
vnguntur : Hi-
eroſolymitanus
Francorum,
Anglorum &
Siculorum : Barti
Caſſaneus, Fol.
127. De Glo-
ria, M. Aſ;
Francorum Rex
Regis Angliæ
eſt Tributarius:
Anglia etiam
Rex , Franciæ,
Legitimo deue-
minatur & in-
ſequitur Tetulo,

in token of their ſyncere and vnfayned making great Account of our
ſound Amitie , and good Peace with them to be continued : In reſpect,
of all the Premiſſes, The forſayd T E N T H of Forrein Fiſhing
(as before) demaunded, and agreed vpon, F O R E V E R :
may ſeme, both, on our behalf, and alſo , on the behalf of all
the honeſt and well aduiſed Forreiners(whom it doth, or ſhall
concern ,) to be very reaſonably , iuſtly, and freendly demaunded, decreed, and accorded vpon, F O R E V E R : That is to ſay,
ſo long tyme , as the ſayd P E T Y N A V Y R O Y A L L , ſhall
enioy, the R O Y A L L S O V E R A I N T Y of the B R Y T I S H
S E A S : according to this firſt Plat , or , ſome better Inſtitu-
tion , thereof .

A Couenant very Iuſt, Freendly , and Commodious, for both Parts.

Yt is alſo to be known and Noted , for our Comfort herein , toward
the Charges of the ſayd Pety-Nauy-Royall : That the Tenth , yeerly, of all Forreyn Fiſhings , within the Sea Limits, to her Maieſties Royalty appropriat, is aboue an Hundred Thouſand
pownds, *de Claro.*

Note.

Good Cumfort of great Importance.

Gwicciardine , in his Deſcription of the Low Cuntry, geueth good
Euidence of one portion therof . As , of our Herring Fiſhing alone:
(what ſay I , Ours ? Nay , the Flemiſh Herring Fiſhings , in our Engliſh or Brytiſh Sea Coaſts.) For , he recordeth , that the Low Cuntries,
make yeerly 490 Thouſand pounds ſterling , of thoſe Herring,
Salted and Barelled : Rebating the Charge of the Salt . By this , you
may haue a gros geſſe , of farder Reconing.

But , how ſoundeth this Latin Record , in a true & diſcrete Brytiſh Subiects eares : either , in reſpect of the los ſuſteyned , in Reuenue : or , in Reſpect of ſome Diſgrace, redounding to them, that can Redres the ſame : yf,
it be amyſſe ? *Eſt etiam eodem* ⁎ *tempore, Copioſiſſima Halecis Piſcatura , in Lit-*
toribus Angliæ & Scotiæ : quæ , per Piſcatores Flandriæ inſtituitur : à qui-
bus poſteà , ſortitur Nomen : vt , Romam ille Piſcis delatus , Halec Flandrorum
appelletur . The ſame Sea, is called *M A R E* ⁎ *B R Y T A N I-*
C V M : And the Sea Coaſts , be called of all Nations likewiſe *L I T-*
T O R A B R Y T A N I Æ , Littora Angliæ : And yet , the
Herring , therin taken , are called *H A L E C F L A N D R O R V M :*
Nay, we our ſelues, call them, Flemyſh Herring : Yea , we our ſelues,
being beaten from our own Fiſhings , and Fiſhing places, are glad to buy
our own Commodity, of Strangers : Againſt all Reaſon , Conſcience,
Law , and good Ciuill Policy.

⁎ *Sub Prin-*
cipio Autŭ-
ni .
Olaus Mag-
nus Lib. 20.
Cap. 28.
⁎ *Albertus*
Krantzius lib
4. cap: 20
Danica Hiſt.
& lib. 1. cap
39 Norm.
Hiſt. &c.

Yt were a ſhame, to allege, that they are woorthy to enioy our Fiſhings , as Lords therof : bycauſe, they can ſkill to handle and order the Herring , better , than Engliſh-men . We muſt take hede of that
                                        Reaſon,

Reafon, betimes : For, fo, they can do our Wooll, and vndreſſed
Cloth : the more wicked or vnſkilfull; are our workmen at home, the
whiles : And the les of our Wooll, and vndreſſed Cloth, wold haue
bin put into their hands, to try ſuch Maiſtries therewith: &c. But, to our
preſent purpofe returning.

Then, By Gods grace, we may (comfortably) thus Anſwere to this
firſt Dowt, In the name of the whole Body Politicall. Seeing, Our Reuenues, now, and wealth, are greater, then was our forefathers: And
Seeing, we are ſufficiently perſwaded of the manifold Publik Benefits, ſuch,
as neuer hapned to our forefathers (for all their Incredible foreſayd great
Charges) And which, by all humayn coniecture, are like to enſue: not
only to our ſelues, but alſo to our Wiues, Children, Kindred, Freends:
And ſo, to this whole Brytiſh Kingdom, vniuerſally: both now, and
euer, after our dayes: We will (ſay we) be found, through Gods help,
ſo well aduiſed, ſo diſcrete, ſo liberall herein, and bountifull, as, aboue all
things, this hoped-for Publik Peace, and Generall Security, chiefly
requireth, that we ſhould be:

And the Hundred Thowſand pounds, all manner of wayes, to
theſe vſes, collected, will amount to be ſo many, as we throughly are
perſwaded: (Theſe laſt diſcourſes, well conſidered: and two more, which
we, of our ſelues, with great reaſon and probability, will annex hereunto)
That, contrary to the firſt dout, we confidently, now, may truſt, that,
not onely, for this Pety Nauy Royall, a ſufficient maſſe of Threaſor,
will eaſily and ſpedily be contributed: But, great * Ouerplus alſo; will
thereof grow (ere long.)

And then, it is intended, That " a Parte therof, ſhall be employed
toward the Relief of ſuch poore Men, as either by Sickues, maym, or vn-
weldynes of age, are to be diſmiſſed from the ſayd Nauy: and other, to
be taken in, in their roomes. " Part, toward the finding of the poore
Widdowes, and Orphanes of ſuch Men, as in good ſeruice, in the ſayd
Nauy, haue manfully ſpent their lyues: " Parte, toward a ſufficient Sti-
pend, for 4 Pety Pylots Publik, in 4 ſundry, and apt Ports of this
Iland, to be reſident, and ready to ſerue, Mathematically and Mechani-
cally, with Quadrants, Rings, Chartes, Sea Compaſſes, Sandglaſſes,
and ſuch other furniture, as to the charge and Seruice of Pylotage, and
Maiſterſhip in the foreſayd Nauy, may be found needfull: each one appoynted to xx Ships: (or a Quarter of the whole Pety Nauy Royall, how
great ſo euer it do grow hereafter:) To thoſe Ships, I mean, that are to
the Coaſts, next him, aſſigned. And thoſe 4 Pylots, Firſt, to be choſen
out of them, that haue, allready, become expert at Sea: And then,
by the Grand-Pylot-generall of England (for the tyme, being) to be
informed farder, as appertayneth: And that, euery yere, once, by their
appointed repayre, made vnto him, at place certayn. Other * parte,
for Preparation of Store, of things neceſſary to the ſayd Nauy: And eche
thing, excellent good, and perfect in his kinde. An other " parte therof, to be beſtowed toward neceſſary Hauens, Harboroughes, Ports;

D.ij.   Block-

The Anſwer to the Firſt Dowbt.

The Politik beſtowing of Some of the Ouer-plus, of the Pety Nauies Threaſor.

Fowre Pety Pilots Publik.

The Grand-Pilot Gene-rall, of Eng-land.

Blockhoufes &c. mainteyning : or, in moft needfull places, new making. And " Parte , in building euery yere , fome excellent Ships of war , for the forefayd Pety Nauy Royall . Some , toward New 7. Forreyn Difcoueries making : for Gods glory, the Wealth-Publik and the Honorable Renown of this Ilandifh Impire . Wherupon , alfo , dependeth the Firft of our two difcourfes, before fpoken of . For , fo may parte of the Threafory of the Pety Nauy Royall , be employed , toward New Difcoueries making, that, of all fuch Difcoueries , the half Charges may be Contributed out of the Threafory of the forefayd Pety Nauy Royall : And fo, likewife , the half clere * Gayn therof comming , to be to the fayd Threafory due , and anfwered accordingly : by like , and like number of Officers , as are for the reft of the Society of fuch Difcoueries .

Foreyn Difcoueries.

10.

Greater Publik Equitie , is in fuch a manner of New Societies making : and with better order , and more ayd , may greater things be attempted , than hitherto haue bin : with the Timerous myndes of a Few : and therefore , with their to to ftraight Allowances , at their firft Onfet giuing . Wherupon (oftentimes) not only their firft Charges haue bin loft : But alfo , the Attempts difcreditted : as of things , either vnlucky, vnlikely , or vntrue : where , none of all thefe points , hath bin the occafion of fuch yll Succes .

By this means , all Marchants, and other , that are Partners of Priuileged voyages , fhall be, not only vnhindred , of their hoped-for Gayn : but , rather, greatly furdred , to bring that to pas , by Publik Ayd , and to the Benefit Publik , and Priuate alfo : which , before , with much adoo , could fcarfe be maiftered : to make them (a few parteners of fuch Societies) to become, Priuately, Welthy thereby .

Note.

Hereuppon alfo , the Queenes Maiefties Cuftomes, both owtward and homeward , will greatly be encreafed : And all the Commons, and Body of the Realm, will grow in greater loue , with the Marchants Dooings : and better like of the Princes eftablifhing of fuch Priuileged Societies : When, the wary and carefull Diligence of the Merchant , and the gracious Priuilege of the Prince, fhall (PROPORTIONALLY) be beneficiall to ONE , A FEW, and ALL . (Which is the chief Mark , that One , a Few , and All , fhold fhote at.) For, fo , fhall fuch Dooings, be afmuch auaylable to the Common-wealth , then , as , now they are to the Priuate Lucre of a Few : And that , with Publik Dammage . Seeing , the felf fame things , which they Bring in , or Deale with , now, be Deerer bought than they were, before any fuch New Trade or Society , therin Priuileged.

¶And in like forte, is to be fayd, in this our Second Difcours, of all other ' Homifh Difcoueries, to be made within the Queenes Maiefties Dominions, of her Brytifh Impire. For, moft certayn yt is, that there is Naturally * couered in the Earth, and vnknown , in thefe Dominions, fo great Riches of Lead, Tyn, Copper, Syluer, Gold, and Diuers kyndes of other very commodious and proffitable Minerall Matters , as might incredibly

11.
Homifh Difcoueries.

credibly encreafe both the Threafor Royall, and alfo of all the Partners Publik and Priuate: who, fhould Proportionally, be at all Charges, about fuch Minerall Difcoueries, to be throwghly and Maifterly
executed.

And by the way : How think you ? Doth it not fting the Naturall
born Subiects, that Strangers fhall be grafted into their places: and their
Publik and priuate Parte of Benefit, to be, thereby Cut of ? The Strangers Science, and Cunning, might be recompenced, and their Charges allowed : But, fo vnnaturally to deale with the True and Naturall Body Politik, yt is not Neceffary : I will fay no farder . And, if Strangers, wold not fo deale, other, wold : and will be found.

This thing, being once, by due Publik order and Authority, eftabli- Note.
fhed : How many an Owre, and Myne, (very rich,) wold be
difclofed and pointed to : Where, they are : and Minerall Examples,
of great Cumfort, fhewed by diuers Priuate Men ? (Ientlemen and other)
who, now, will neuer open their Mouthes, to difclofe the fame : Bycaufe, in their own Grounds, where their Propriety (by Gods law, and
the Law of Nature) fhould be, to them, moft benefitiall of all other
Men : now, (as the manner, yet, is) their parte, wold be leaft, of all
other.

But, when, with better Allowance to the Prince, and the Proprie- Note
tary Owner of the Soyle alfo, (where any Gayn may rife by Myning)
and with fome great Publik Commodity (as to the Threafory of the
Pety Nauy Royall,) thefe Minerall and Mettall woorks, fhall be followed; * Then, Priuate Men, will not grudge, though 40, or an hun- Then
dred other Priuate Partners, haue great Gayn of their peculiar ground.
And therupon (Say we) the Commodity, all manner of wayes, will arife ☞
greater, than euer it will do, otherwife, by fuch Societies, as they
now are.

And vpon this Confideration, that, of their Perpetuall Beneuolence, for Sea Security, Some portion therof, fhall be employed to
fuch Publik vfes, as both the whole Body of the Realm, may vndou-
tedly haue fome fenfible and certayn proof, that their Publik Threa- The Induftrious Encreafing of the PVBLIK THREASORY, is A Principall Cumfort to the Commons.
fory of the Pety Nauy Royall, doth, as proportionally encreafe, as a-
ny, or a few Priuate Mens Coffers els, before, were, or (by good order) mought haue bin, by fuch Societies, well amended : vpon this Confideration (Say we) How gladly, and how readily, will euery Man ☞
be Contributer therunto, after the moft eafy Rate, and proportion prefcribed ? And making this Reconing among them felues, (ouer and befides
all the former marueilous great Benefits Publik, rehearfed :) Thus, will
they, then, fay : Yea Mary : This, is Common-wealth like, in *The Frank Speche of the wifer fort of the Community.
dede : When, our Common Threafory, is as carefully, and dif-
creetly augmented, by the wifdom and Authority of the Higher Magi-
ftrates, and the witty and Circumfpect trauailes of our Parteners, (Marchants

chants, and other, whofoeuer) As, before, by fuch Priuileges, All, was intended and procured for the Benefit onely of a few . And chiefly, Seeing, before, the gaynfull wares and things, wherof they were Parteners, were, by their vnhabilities (not infatiable Couetoufnes) that dealt with thofe Attempts : or by the manner, as they dealt with them , become very dere : and derer , than before fuch their Societies eftablifhed . Reafon perfect none can be yelded, why it fhould fo be : But, this Single foule Allegation, is often repeated : The great Charges, which hitherto haue byn layd on their Shoulders, in that peculiar Trade of their Society . &c . And therfore, affone as they are in poffeffion of any thing , to raife Mony on : they think it politikly done , to make prefently their Reconing of their whole Charges hitherto fufteyned : And fo, by and by, to begyn to raife the pryces of their things, higher, than they found them, before their new Societies erected : to haften, thereby,

☞ their difcharge, or Recompence of Dammages (fay they) as yet fufteyned . And fo, by that means, the poore Commons, buying the fame wares derer, than before : become (feely Soules) Contributers to thefe few Mens priuate wealth amending : But, to the decaying and weakening of the wealth and hability of the Commons.

And therfore, by the prefcript of humayn Reafon, yt is a more perfect Politicall Ordonance, fo, before hand to eafe all fuch difordered Charges, that, both, Rich *[1] Forreyn New Trades, and great

Threafor, may fubftancially and throughly be brought in , and purchafed to this Kingdom : publikly, as well, as priuatly : And alfo, that Gods great Bountifulnes, *[2] Couertly beftowed vpon this Incomparable Ilandifh Monarchy, may, by Publik Ayde alfo, be fo brought to light, handling, and vfe, as the whole Commons, hereby, may in their Pety Nauy Threafor, become wealthyer : And pryces of fuch things as (either

☞ one way, or the other) are gotten : may be either kept low, or brought low : That, the greateft parte of this Kingdom, (which are the poorer fort) may, both, laude and bles God, for the wifdom, Charity, and Iuftice, of their Gouernors (Wherupon alfo, they will both better loue them : And for very loue, be more affrayd, to difpleafe them .) And alfo, vniuerfally, all the Realm ouer, the true and faithfull Bleffing and prayer of all honeft Subiects, may be concurrent with, and affiftant to, all fuch honorable and Publik Attempts, either 1 Forreyn

or 2 Homifh : for the better fucces therof obtaining, by Gods mercy : wherewith, thefe our two brief Difcourfes, in this place, fhall be finifhed.

These Ten Generall, and Extraordinary means ,
of increafing the Threafory of the Pety Nauy
Royall, in this place, may be thought
fufficient, for the probable Diffoluing of the firft Dowt.

And, as for the fecond Obiection, yt is more eafy and certayn, to put to put that point, owt of all Dowt. I mean, as Concerning Scarfity, and Dearth, of Vittailes, fufpected or Dowted, by the continuall vittailing of this Nauy. Mary, herein, fome forecaft muft be vfed: as, fundry other, in other points, are. (But not * here to be rehearfed.)

For, as the Men, to Furnifh the forfayd Nauy with, are to be chofen, (and that, with Diuers Confiderations) owt of all Shires, and Coafts of this Realm of England: So, likewife, the vittailes, are, fo, to be prouided for, that the whole Realm, may yelde the fame: euery parte, according to the fertility of the Soyle: And according to the Store to be referued, for their Seruice, actuall or poffible, otherwife. And that is very needfull: yf, againft forreyn Enemy, we fhould nede a Mayn Army (one, or mo,) by land, any way, toward Coaft or Border: or, for the Grand Nauy Royall vittailing; in tyme of nede.

And, feeing the Vittailes, fhall be fo indifferently, or proportionally prepared, all the Realm ouer (as before,) How can any one party, in this Publik, and Common-wealths Cafe, finde him felf ftraightly, vnduly, or vuiuftly, dealt withall?

And, as the Vittailes, and Men, fhould rife, (after a fort) ioyntly and proportionally, within the places correfpondent: Store alwayes to be referued: as I fayd: (And fuch, about the Riuer of Thames chiefly, and within certayn myles therof, And in other Quarters: as, both for the City of London, continually: And the Grand Nauy Royall, in tyme ofnede, may be [as it hath bin] feruifable:) So, fhould the Ships, receiue thofe Men and Vittayles in, at Twenty fundry Places, or Ports, in England.

Now, feeing then, this Vittayle, thus orderly and indifferently prepared, out of all Places, is to be beftowed on * Chriften-men: yea, and them, our own * Cuntrymen: And not, on FORREYNER, SCOT, FRENCH, FLEMISH, DANE, or SPANIARD, &c. And fome of them, either Sonnes, * or Brothers, or Fathers, or Cofens, or Kinfemen, or Singular Freends! Yea, fome, Efquyers, fome Knights, fome Barons: And fome of them; Landlords, to fundry of vs at home; here remayning: * Fourthly, Seeing, this Vittaile is to be beftowed on them, who do, and will aduenture their lyues, in all Cafualties and dangers of the Sea: And againft all violence of Pyrate, or any open warryor! And that, not, for any their own Priuate Quarrell: But for the Publik Safety, and Security, of all England and Ireland. Not, for thyne, and myne, alone: But, for the Safegard and profperous Eftate, of Millions of Men, Women, and Children, within this Monarchy; on Land: (and by this means,) at their eafe, quyet, and pleafure, remayning. Confidering then, well and erneftly, all thofe 4 generall Refpects.: What true and Sound member, is there, of this Common wealth: and faithfull defirer of the bleffed Peaceable Security, of England and Ireland, vnder our Souerayn Empres, our moft Gracious Elizabeth: who, will not (in a manner) be willing, the Charges to be

borne

This brief Adtertifemét doth expres but fome of the principall poynts, moft behoofull for the Common-Wealth at this tyme.

Note this Poynt.

The Twenty Ports for the Pety Nauy Royall.

* 1.
* 2.
* 3.

* 4.

borne (parte and parte like) the whole Realm throughout ? wherewith, to bestow meate and drink, on them , continually : that refuse no one day, or a moment (yf occasion be offred) to aduenture their hart blud , lyfe, and Lymmes , for vs : And on Seaboord, continually, to endure hard dyet and lodging : for Commodities innumerable , of both thefe whole Kingdoms ?

☞ But, it is not fo meant: as, to haue any farder Contribution of purs , then is before fpoken of . But, what is he, (Yea, what is he, I fay agayn ?) is he, a found member of the Common-wealth : a faithfull Subiect to our good Queene Elizabeth : or, a Charitable Chriftian, that either wold (in this Common wealths feruice, or at any tyme els) * hide Corn, or other vittayle, from Publik Ayde, and Reliefes : Or els , wold not be content, to receiue the due value, and reafonable Pryce therof , very gladly ? But , moft miferably, wretchedly , couetuoufly, yea vnchriftianly, (I will not fay, Trayterously) wold defire (now chiefly) to en-hance the price of Corn, and Vittayles, to the great pinching of the poore at home: And perchance, for a Trayterous means, to hinder the vittayling of the forefayd Pety-Nauy-Royall : or, to make it odious, or doutfully thought of, to fome : as though , it were a iuft occafion , of prices of Corn and vittayles ftarting vp : more now, then before? O, vayn, blynde, Couetous Mifer (who fo euer he be , that is fo mynded.) Thou , and thy like , and that of late dayes, when no Army, or Nauy, hath bin to be vit-tayled, haft, on the fudden, and in the tyme of great Store, all the Realm ouer, (euen then) God knoweth, vpon what wicked Intent , or mifcon-ftruing , for light Credit geuing to Coniecture, found in fome new Three halfpeny Prognoftication: haft, moft vnreafonably enhaunfed the Prices of Corn, Butter and Chefe: And at other tymes, of Beofs, and Muttons, &c.

I Pray thee, be Reafonable : and think truly : and make Reckening with me, Chriftianlike : and like a good Member of this Common Wealth: And, as a true Subiect, to our Souerayn.

What, may be the * true caufe, of Dearth (whenfoeuer it pleafeth God, to vfe that his fkourge?) Any other thing, but Want of Corne, or Vittayles ? That Want, yf God fend yt, is eyther by the Ordinary Cau-fes Naturall, taking effect, according to the Predeftined Plat of this whole wordls *oeconomie*, and contynuance : Or, it is, by Extraordinary Means, of Gods fending : And that, Diuerfly, and in diuers tymes, and States of the Corne, or Cattayle &c. Thefe, be true Dearths, vpon great wants of Corn, or Cattayle to be had : Or, at the leaft, to be had fo good, as is behoofull for Mans bodily Suftenance? All other Dearths , that come not of Want, by Diuine means : are ei-ther by "- Fraudulent Want : As, through Corne, and Vittayles ftolne, and Priuily conueyed to our Enemyes, or Fickle freends : for Priuate gayn only : to the hinderance of the Wealth-publik : Or, by falfly ·· Pretended Want : As the Vnchriftianlike Practife, of fuch Caterpillers, and Raue-ning Wolues : (Deuouring Corne and Cattell) wold make the Commons beleue. And, when, Abundance and Sufficiency is, to make and Wraft a Dearth: by felling Three Quarters of Wheat, of the very value (then) of Fowr:

Margin notes:

☞

* *Solomon Prouerb. 11. Qui abfcon-dit Frumen-ta, maledice-tur in populis: Benedictio autem fuper Caput Ven-dentium .*

☞

The true Caufe of Dearth.

of fowr : And Three Oxen , of the very value of fowr : and so , of Shepe
&c . What a Deuouring , and Rauening , is this ? Of euery Fowr , to De -
voure and consume one : and the same , neuer more to be hard of , in this
Common-Wealth ? And this , only , for his most Priuate Gaynes sake , to
be Bagged , or Chested vp , for his Idoll , to behold or Delight in , As in
his strength , and furniture : ready to mainteyn hym ; in other wicked
purposes : And (as God knoweth) foolish Intents . Perchance ; with some
of that pelf (so miserably and diuelishly scraped together , or violently , in
manner , wrasted out of the poore Commons hands , and mouthes) to be
at Charges , to enclose some parte of the Commons , from a poore   Common
Village , or Township . With some , to buy his neighbours House , or   Enclosing:
Farme , ouer his hed : and so ; to make him freends , of the Mammon of
Iniquity . Nay , Nay , make him self , the Carefull freend , and doting louer ,
of wicked Mammon : The Diuell Infernall , and not of God , nor his
Members : Nor the members of the Common-wealth : Yea ; many a
Thousand of such , as , eche one of them , is more profitable and Com-
fortable to the Weal-Publik of England , than a Thousand such Mam-
mons dearlings are . I mean the Maryner , the Soldyer , the Ientleman ,
Esquyer , and Knight , yea and Baron : now , Tost and Turmoyled at Seas :
being the Publik Watchmen , Garde , and Champions , for the most Blesse
sed State of Traquillity publik , in this Sacred Monarchy , preseruing.

     And no les , is the Error and disorder vsed in this Kingdom ; of *Dar-*
danarie Trade , and *Monopolie* : two greuous hindrances , to the Weale-
Publik . *Iacobus Simancas* , *Episcopus Pacensis* , sayd very well , in his book   A⁴ 1570;
De Republica : * dedicated to the King of Spayn . *Ne oneretur Annona, &*   Agaiſt our
ideo rerum Vanalium Pretia , iniqua sint : animaduertere oportet in DARDA- English To To;
NARIOS , qui omnia præemunt ; vt ea postea Carius vendant . Hi many Dardana-
quidem perniciosissimi Rebus-publicis esse solent : Vtpote genus auarum , & iniu- ries:
sti Lucri Cupidissimum .   And again.   You may al-
   so in *Vlpian*.
     Multis quoq, legibus Regijs Occursum est Dardanarijs . *Sed illa , omnium est* (*Lib . 47 .*
optima , & Rebus-publicis vtilissima , quæ vetat , Ne quisquam vnquam fru- ff . Tit . 11)
mentum emat , vt vendat : Ea enim effectum est , vt res frumentaria , iustis Finde Confi-
pratijs vendatur , & vilitas Annonæ Consecuta sit . Quanobrem , plurimum Reipu- deration a-
blicæ interest , vt ea Lex Conseruetur : & qui secus fecerit , acerrimè coerceatur . gainst Dar-
   dinaries .
     And as for *MONOPOLIE* : this , had the same *Simancas* Noted , out of
Zeno his Constitutions .   *Lib . 4. C*
   Tit . 59.
     Iubemus , ne quis cuiuscunq, Vestis , vel Piscis , vel cuiuslibet alterius ad victum ,
vel ad quemcunq, vsum pertinentis Species , Monopolium audeat exercere : Ne-
ue quis , illicitis habitis Conuentionibus , Coniurare , aut pacisci , vt Species diuer-
sorum Corporum negociationis , non minoris quàm inter se statuerint , venunden-
tur . Ædificiorum quoq, artifices , aliorumq, diuersorum Operum professores , pęni-
tus arceantur , pacta inter se Componere ; vt ea quis , quod alteri commissum sit ,
Opus , impleat : aut iniuncta alteri solicitudinem , alter intercipiat . Si quis au-
tem MONOPOLIVM ausus fuerit exercere , bonis proprijs expo-
liatus , perpetuitate damnetur Exilij .
     Agayn ; what Reason hath any Man to go about , by raysing pryce
       E2   of vittayles;

of vittayles, to brede opinion in fome fimple heds , that this Nauy , is occafion therof : And fo , to caufe mifliking of that, by one mean : which by his former Publik Contribution , he pretendeth to be glad and defi-rous , that it fhould continually be well mainteyned ? What dubble and

hypocriticall dealing were that ? * With one hand , to offer Bread : and in the other , to hold a Stone , ready to geue a blow therwith , to the Receiuer of that bread ? All fuch forts, of Fraudulently or Violently cau-fed Dearths, as , they are very much againft the Common-wealth , and Common Comfort, (to be receiued of Gods mercifull Plenty, or Suffici-ency of Corn and Vittayles fent vs :) So, will they now , (as the poore Commons are in good hope) either , for very Confcience fake : Or , for good zeales fake , to the due and Reafonable maintenance , of the forefayd Pety-Nauy-Royall, be vtterly abhorred , efchewed , and very well left .

1 . And here , alfo , the poore Commons wold(yf they Durft) make

Supplication, All , kneeling on Knees, Man , Woman, and Childe : and ioyntly, with one moft humble Voyce, Requeft the Higher Powers, That No more Vittayles (Corn , or other ,) might, vnder Licence , (or cullor therof,) be Tranfported to Forreyners : or otherwife , (in this Realme) by Priuilege to be vfed : Than, as may be beft, to the Publik-be-hoof of all them at home , and for the fufficient and more eafy Mayn-tenance, of thofe Valiant & worthy Publik Watchmen, lying owt at Seas.

2 . ¶And, furdermore , that in tyme of Excellent Plenty , and good cheap : the Ouerplus of Corn, and other vittayles , may be brought to the next

Publik Garners and Stoarhowfes , being at , or nere vnto , the forefayd Twenty Ports, to the Pety Nauy Royall, affigned . And there, with Publik Mony of the Pety Nauy his Threafor , to be payd for , prefently :

3 . And from thofe 20 Garners, or Stoarhoufes , only , to be , to places conuenient ✳ Tranfportable : vnder the Generall * Licence, from her Maiefty, before, graunted vnto the Body of the Pety Counfaill, of chief Officers , to the Pety-Nauy-Royall appointed .

4 . ¶And wold , alfo, make humble Requeft, that the Incredible Abufes of Purueyers , and Takers of vittayles , and other things , might be more nar-rowly fene to , and duly reformed .

5. And Fifthly, the felffame Brytifh and Englifh Commons, Man, Woman , and Childe , with wringing hands , moft pitifully lamenting a Remediles Inconuenience , and haynous Abfurdity , already , and to long, committed : wold , moft humbly and durifully, make Petition , that Pre-

fently , fuch vnparciall prouidence may be vfed : *That, from hence-foorth, The Priuate Commodity of a few , fhall not caufe the Braynes of many a thoufand, of true and faithfull Englifh Subiects, to fly in the Ayre . Braynes (fay they) Armes , Leggs, Lymmes , and lyues of the Commons , to be (as the Cafe may fall out, which , God forbid ,) folde after a fort : Though , not directly , and wil-lingly : yet Indirectly & vnwillingly (in refpect of our Cuntry-mens Intents therin :) Seeing the Chiefeft Inftruments , wherewith to work fo wo-

full

full a Spoyle and Calamity, are dayly (almoſt) from this Kingdom conueyed; (No, no, it goeth not ſo nycely to woork: For, open Markets and
Sales, are made of them, in great plenty) to ſuch Copemens hands, as,
No one of them, doth hartily, and will conſtantly, or can perpetually,
with our proſperous eſtate. Nay, ſuch, as, for many yeres, (almoſt continually) ſome of them, haue gone about, to ouerthrow, and confound,
this bleſſed Brytiſh Monarchy : And ſome of them, ſuch a Nation,
whoſe Records, Chronicles, and Hiſtories, both Ancient, and of late
dayes, publiſhed, do term Engliſh-men, Their Ancient Enemies:
And, in dede, in hart, do erneſtly deſire, and conſtantly * Hope, one
day, to handle them ſo : What thouſand crouching Salutations ſo euer,
(with *Monſieur*, and, *A Voſtre Commandement*, *Monſieur* : and the like
appertenances) of glorious gloſing, and depe diſſimulation, their great
Neceſſity (at any tyme) teacheth them to deuiſe, and counterfet. A true
Leſſon, this Olde Prouerb, will be found, in Such : That, which is
bred in the Bone, will neuer out of the fleſh.

  - Good God, who knoweth not, what *Prouiſo* is made and kept, in o-
ther Common-Weales, Againſt Armour carrying out of their Limits ?
* Such, and to ſuch Places, chiefly, from which, (poſſibly) they may,
thereby, receiue great dammage. And ſhall we, with the moſt terri-
ble, forcible, and hurtfull kynde of Weapon, and Engyn, furniſh both
the Infidels, and the Barbarous Princes forreyn, (though, far from vs, yet
to the deſtruction of Chriſtians, notwithſtanding.) And alſo, nere at
hand, ſuch kynde of people, as, (which way ſo euer, the matters
in controuerſy, fall out, finally) will be found, an Incredible great
Scourge, to this Kingdom, by vnſuſpected means : as the wofull Commons, make their pitifull Reconing, already : or greatly do dout : how
rude, ſo euer, ſome of theſe people, of them ſelues, be : And how ſimple and ſlender ſo euer, their preſently ſene, and known Nauy, is to be
regarded.

  Therfore, if the Brytiſh Communnalty, may obteyn ſo much
Grace at our Souerayn., and her moſt Honorable Priuy Counſailes hands:
As, to enioy the Benefit of Sea-Security, by means of the foreſayd Pety-Nauy-Royall : Then, ſuch Caſt-Peces of Iren Ordinances,
we ſhall greatly nede, for our own Ships furniture : And alſo,
other *Iren* works, diuers wayes. Fewell alſo, and Ship Tymber (from
tyme to tyme) we ſhall haue occaſion to vſe, more, then els, wold be occupyed. And then, the want of ſo many Hundred Peces (of *Iren*
we mean, and not, of Bras to,) as haue bin, of late, from hens tranſported, will make very euident, the Dubble Dammage, and Treble Danger, poſſibly, enſuing therof, when, our Enemies, being with our Store
furniſhed, we muſt be conſtrayned to prouide the like, new : and ſo, be
driuen to tarry a great tyme. And alſo, to take the fortune of all faults,
In *Iren* Peces, happening. Whereas, otherwiſe, at leyſure, the Principall good Peeces (in all Reſpects) heretofore, continually cuſſed out:
And, In * Rupe Tarpeia, of our New Troy, reſerued, thought (without

E.iſ.

* Though our
Frendes may
Reaſonably be
thought wor-
thy to be Hol-
pen With Ar-
mour, againſt
our Common
Enemy. Yet vn-
der pretence of
ſuch Freendly
Dealing, The
Common Ene-
my is not to be
Furniſhed here-
with, as Plen-
tifully, as, ey-
ther his Caſe re
quireth, or his
Purſe is hable
to reach vnto.
Wherof the
Right Hono-
rable Priuy
Counſaile haue
very Wiſely
geuen warning
to the Contra-
ry. And the
lyke Conſidera-
tion, is to be
had, for Vit-
tayles Tranſ-
porting.

(without any detriment to the Prince or Commons) haue now ferued our turns very well : And fo , the Poore Commons fhould not haue , One , and the fame Awle , twife thruft in their right Eyes . As , to fee , and fele agayn , the Incredible Spoyle of Woods , and Forefts , as hath bin made , to furder Iren works withall : And yet , (Notwithftanding ,) Iren to be now , derer , than it was , when , from beyond the Seas , we were chiefly ferued therof : And our Iren alfo (yet) worfe , then the forreyn I-ren . And our Woods , and Forefts , already , fo deftroyed thereby , that Fewell , and Tymber , of all forts , (of neceffity) in many places of this Realm , is become , on the fudden , extremely dere : and therupon , * Pryces of vittayles , fomwhat the higher rayfed.

> *The Prices of Vittayles, en-hanced, by in-direct means.

Oh , the Lamentable Spoyle of our woods , fundry wayes : both , contrary to Lawes made , and alfo , for lack of fufficient *Prouifo* , and due execution , as wifely and iuftly performed , as either Olde Lawes made , or new , deuifed , was , and may be , a fufficient Token of wifdom Speculatiue , in Lawmakers heds : But the great Rechelefnes , in the Practife (which onely , fhould be the great Profit to the Common-Wealth , expe-cted) doth make vs feme great Hypocrites : in good Lawes making : and keping the Bookes , wherein , the Lawes are recorded : but not obferuing the Lawes , in our Actions Ciuile.

> *Omnis Laus Vertutis, in Actione Con-fiftit. Arift.*

Peraduenture , yf (among fundry other Ordonances , for preferua-tion of Wood and Tymber , to be made) fome *Prouifo* were eftablifhed , by Act of Parlement , that No man fhould Buyld , or caufe to be Buylt , but with thefe Three poynts , concurring : First , according to his Ha-bilitie , and not aboue : Secondly , according to his State , or Voca-tion , and not aboue : Thirdly , according as his Neceffary Affaires , and allowable Commodities , fhall require , and not Superfluoufly : Ther-upon , fewer Banckrupts , and more Houfe-keepers , would be found : Les Ambition , and more Charitie , wold be vfed : And , Thirdly , bet-ter Cheap of more Store and Choyce of Ship-Tymber , and other , wold be referued.

> A Nedefull Prouifo, againft Vnhable, Vn-decent, or Su-perfluous Buyl-ders.

> The Commodi-ties, of this Pro-uifo.

The Penalties of the former Tranfgreffors , might be , after this , or , a better manner , Decreed . Of the First , the Houfe and Houfes , fo built , to be fold , by Auction : And the Tenth parte of the Whole Va-lue , to be contributed , to the Threafory of the Pety-Nauy-Royall . And the other Nyne partes , to be payd to the Creditors : to euery Man , proportionally : fo far , as the fame Auction-Mony will reach : And , yf there be any Ouerplus remayning , the fame , to be reftored to the fayd Offender . Of the Second , the Houfe and Houfes , to be duely valued : And the Fifth Parte , of the Whole Value , to be immediatly Payable : the one half therof , to the Queenes Maieftie her Exchecquer : and the other half therof , to the Threafory of the Pety-Nauy-Royall . Of the Third , the valuation of the Superfluous Houfes , or other Buildings , (beeing duly eftimated and rated :) the Twentith parte therof , to be forfetted to her Highnes Threafory , onely.

> The Penalties of thefe three manner of Dif-orderly Buyl-ders.
> 1.
> 2.
> 3.

Out of which Three manner of Forfets , and Amercements , the Fifth parte of the Forfet , is to be awarded due to him , or them , who truly

do

do geue Aduertisement of the sayd Disorder : and sufficiently doth proue
the same , so to be, as his Aduertisement specifieth .

  Now then , how can it stand with the Termes of good Policy , All
these great Incommodities Publik , depending vpon our greatly disordred
Iren Mynes: And yet, notwithstanding, such Warlike prouision, as ; so Dere- **D**
ly to the Commons, is wrought and made therof : For a fewe Mens
priuat commodity (we know not whom) to be caryed away ;
far and nere : to our great dissurnishing : And to the furniture and
Strengthning of Moore or Moschouite : or other Forreyn Prince: French
or Fleming : our Secret Mortall Foes, or vnassured Freends ? In effect:
The Sorrowfull Commons , most hartily wishing the Pety-Nauy-Royall, to be duly mainteyned : And most assured ; that thereto , will be requisite , not onely , Stoare of such Iren Cast Peees , * But also, of Tymber ; **D** * The Occasion
Fewell, and other Iren worke : (The * pryces of all which , being by the & due Reason ;
foresayd disorders , vnreasonably enhaunsed) do greatly dout ; that either of this Petition.
the foresayd things ; will , (by farther disorder ;) become deerer , then they
now are : Or els ; the Extremity of the pryces, being, then , made more
sensible : the simple Multitude , or some other wrangling head, will Impute **D**
all ; to this new deuised Policy, of the Pety-Nauy-Royall mainteyning.
And therfore, in this place of Consideration of Pryces and Dearth, they
wold haue had such a Petition (as before) most humbly moued , to the
higher States . But no one man dare, (I know no iust cause why) vtter ; * The Vnfayned
in * Durifull order, the Tenor of the Premisses , to the higher powers: Zeale of the
Though , (disorderly) many Thousands do murmur at the matter, in mar- Publik Com-
ueilous manner : when , dayly , they finde so many Camps (as it were) modities , Will
of Iren Peeces , ready layd to the Forreyn Market : and for Forreyn Na- Animate the
uyes , or Forts furnishing . Deliuering (thereby) a Rod ; of our own making, Faythfull Sub-
into the hands of them ; who could finde in their harts, to skourge vs with iect to make
wyer whips , as God best knoweth : And to bring vs , into farder Incon- humble Petiti-
ueniences, then, either Dearth of Tymber, Fewell, Iren, or Victayles, are on for Redres
to be esteemed . But, vnto God his most Mercifull and Mighty hands , we of great Enor-
commit our principall Protection, now and euer : mities, as yet ;

  And Suerly, yf there be any Brytish, or English * Pericles, * Yf Pericles
now lyuing, who conueniently may, and will, both Zealously take to hart, *Pericles* be
and also Circumspectly, and depely looke into these, and like Matters: (No- dead, pore
thing fawning vpon Forreyners, Nor to much listening or leaning to their *Plebe* (as a
Aduises, or Deuises, best for them selues, and their Purposes : and not Passager in
for vs, and Ours : Nor fearing Forreyn, or Homish hurt, therefore : the Ship of
Meaning none, him self) He wolde not make Strange ; though the the Com-
weaker and Imperfecter sorte of People (Which are so noosseled and em- mon-welth)
broyed vp to the elbowes , Yea, to their hart rootes , with the Insatiable By leaue,
loue, of To to Priuate Lucre , that, therefore, they care ; To to doth vtter
little, for the Publik and Common-Weale,) He would not (I say) his Faithfull
be Agast, though such wolde Diuilishly Maligne hym , and Subtily seke Care, to the
his Discredit ; and Confusion: as (in deede) the *Atheniensiens*, and other, Helm-man,
did, to good *Pericles*, and other, his like . Yet, for all that, such A *Pe-* *Infra, Pag.*
ricles, wold goe forward, so long , as he might preuayle : obseruing the 69.

         E.iij.   wise

wife Precepts , of Perfect Politik Gouernment . And to fuch, as fownd them felues greued, by any their Priuate Payne, Hurt, Los, or Chardge, fufteyned, by meanes of his Direction or Cownfaill, for Dutifull, and Nedefull Seruice, to be done, to and for the Common-Wealth, either *Militando*, or, *Contribuendo*, or otherwife, he wold fay thus: (For , fo, fayd the True Pericles :)

Thucid.
Lib. 2.

Non eft mihi inexpectata Indignatio Veftra . Intellexi enim me accufari: e-amq, ob caufam, Vos conuocaui : vt vos admoneam, & reprehendam : Si vel mihi Succenfetis, vel Rebus Aduerfis fuccumbitis . Ego enim Iudico, Florente Patria, melius effe Priuatis : quàm Florentibus Priuatis : in afflicta Repub : Nam, etiamfi Priuatus tenet Opes, tamen Euerfa Patria, fimul hac omnia pereunt : Sed in Florente Patria, etiam Pauper Ciuis, faluus effe poteft . Quando igitur, Ciuitas, Priuatorum Ciuium Difficultates fuftinere Poteft : Nemo autem Priuatus vnus, Rempub. Laborantem Suftentare poteft : Juftum eft, Vniuerfos Ei, opem ferre : Et non (quod vos nunc facitis)Perterritos Priuatis Jacturis, deferere REMPVBLICAM.

And in the fame Oration.

Omnibus autem Imperantibus accidit, vt In prafentia, in odio fint . Praclarè autem facit, qui Inuidiam propter Res Honeftas & magnas perfert . Odia autem, non funt perpetua : Sed prafentem Splendorem, fequitur aterna Gloria .

And agayn:

Vos exiftimatis, tantùm Socijs, vos Imperare . Ego autem affirmo , cùm dua partes Bellantibus vfui fint, TERRA, & MARE : Vos, prorfus

Of What Im portance it is, To be Lordr of the Seas .

Maris Dominos effe : & eius partis Cui nunc Imperatis, & Reliqui Maris : SI HAC CLASSE, quam habetis, PROCEDERE VOLVERITIS. Nec ullus Regum, nec ulla Gens, impedire vos in Mari poteft.

In the ATHENIENSIEN STATE, then, yf that were True, Much more, may the BRYTISH IMPIRE Verifie that worde, abfolutely, NOW.

O ALBION, O BRYTAN, O ENGLAND, and (I fay) O BRYTAN, agayn : What is to be hoped, of the Races of thofe thy true Noble Courages : fraught with wifdom and valiantnes : whofe worthy Fame (moft certainly) is regiftred all the world ouer? God forbid, that it fhould truely be fayd: that Onely now, in our days, None can, None may, None dare : or None will, Carefully, and Faithfully vndertake to do fo due feruice to God, fo Beneficiall to this Impire, fo victorious an exploit for his own Immortall Renown eftablifhing, as, to Merite fome parte of a Præface to the Memoriall of his Triumphant Stile, fuch, as the Romane *Pompeius Magnus*, did iuftly deferue, in the Romane Impire.   Which, with thefe

Plin. Lib. 7
Cap. 26.

wordes, by * *Plinie* is diligently recorded: and for euer (thereby) and Gratefully remembred:

CVM

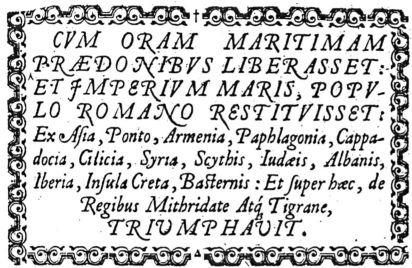

CVM ORAM MARITIMAM PRÆDONIBVS LIBERASSET: ET IMPERIVM MARIS, POPVLO ROMANO RESTITVISSET: Ex Asia, Ponto, Armenia, Paphlagonia, Cappadocia, Cilicia, Syria, Scythis, Iudæis, Albanis, Iberia, Insula Creta, Basternis : Et super hæc, de Regibus Mithridate Atq́ Tigrane, TRIVMPHAVIT.

Oh, Note. What was the Actuall Præface, and politik preparatiue to all these Triumphes? Was it any other, than, *IMPERIVM MARIS, POPVLO ROMANO RESTITVTVM?*

God graunt vs (therfore) the verity and frute, of this Sea Souerainty, euery way: And that, with all Oportunity.

To Conclude then, (In this poynt Answering:) And to end my Conference, with that kinde of People, which either delight in Dearth of Gods sending: or vse (nay abuse.) Dearth Fraudulently procured by other: Or, will them selues Violently force in, And Counterfet a Dearth: And all, for Priuate Lucre onely: (which is a poyson to the Body-Politik of this Kingdom) To those, I confidently affirme: And, Euident and sure it is, that the Mayntenance of the Pety-Nauy-Royall, can cause no one Grayn, or any one pound of Beof, Butter, or Chese: Or any quantity of any other vittayle, to be wanting in this Kingdom: No more, than yf no such Nauy, were to be vittayled.

Note the Reasons, wherfore the Vittayling of the Pety-Nauy-Royall can Cause no Dearth of Vittailes.

And the Reason is: No more Men, are now fed at Sea, thereby, than (yf no such Nauy were) should and wold be fedd at Land. And the little diuersity, and Changing of the place, of the eating of it (As from Land, to Sea) ys not the Cause of any great want: And therfore, (by Reason, afore declared,) no Iust cause, of any Dearth, thereby growing.

1.

Secondly, the Vittayles are so Proportionally, and discretely from all Quarters and Partes of this Kingdom prouided: and so orderly serued in, as no one Corner therof, is, thereby molested, or left destitute of Corn or vittayle: otherwise, than by their own Iudgements, may very well, at that place (to so good vse) be forborne.

2.

Thirdly, True and speedy Publik Payment also, will help to pleasure many Farmars, and other: and be a means, of better cheape buying, commonly. But, olde Custome, yll vsed, of *Debentur Bjlls*, their ouerlong delayed discharge, shall (here) vtterly be abolished.

1.

E.iiij. Fourthly,

Fourthly , the Plenty of former yeres being (by Princely * Priui-
ledge) duly prouided, and diſcretely ſaued, and ordered, in our Twenty
Publik Store-houſes and Garners, of the Pety-Nauy-Royall, may
in tyme of True Dearth , not onely be a marueilous caſe to this Realm,
for the chief Charge of maintayning ſo many Thouſand Engliſh or Brytiſh Subiects, as appertayn to the Pety-Nauy-Royall : But alſo (by
very good reaſon) may be deemed, charitably and politikly made ready:
to be ſeruiſable, for the relief, of many an Hundred of the poore Commons
at home : And that , for pryces, tolerable. I mean, the ſayd Store-houſes,
to be peculiarly ſeruiſable : euery one of them , to ſuch places , chiefly,
as do lye moſt commodiouſly , or next vnto them , to receiue the ſame.
From ſome of which places, before (Ordinarily, and in the tyme of Plenty) parte of the Publik Prouiſion , was gathered into the ſayd Garners,
or Store-houſes . Which manner of pleaſuring the Commons , is very
Charitable Iuſtice.

Fifthly , by the Continuall Sea-Circuits, of this Pety-Nauy-Royall duly vſed) we ſhall, '· Either, at Sea, be a Terror or Bar , to ſuch,
as els (abhominably) wold conuey out of this Kingdom , the Publik Relief of diuers ſortes of Vittayles . So that, they will not (henſſorward)
lightly attempt that their wicked deſire : And thereby , the Commons
may the longer tyme (within the Realm) enioy the frute of Publik Plenty,
lately before floriſhing: ‣ Or, if any (notwithſtanding the vigilant Garde
and Circumſpection of our Pety-Nauy-Royall, in euery Coaſt of this
Realm) will be ſo diueiiſhly aduenturous , as moſt deteſtably to diſfurniſh
this Land of the Vittayles : euen then, moſt nedefull (and alwayes by God
Nature, and Humayn Induſtry, appropriat , to this Kingdom;) Vndoutedly , we ſhall very eaſily intercept, and at Sea, ſeaſon vpon the conueyed
Corn , Butter, Cheſe, Bacon, Barells or Hogſheds of Beof in Powlder,
&c . of ſuch wilfull Offenders : being, (by Mans Law, and all good Conſcience,) forſetted and loſt, from the late lewd Owners thereof . And
then , the ſayd Prouiſion , ſo forſayted , may at the pleaſure and order of
the Queene her moſt excellent Maieſty , and her honorable Priuy Counſaill , be diſtributed by reaſonable ſale , into that parte , or partes of this
Realm, which is known (at that inſtant) to be moſt deſtitute . And where,
alſo , the Publik Garners, and appropriated Store-houſes of the Pety-
Nauy-Royall, can not conueniendy (or, of all the Twenty , the leaſt
conueniendy) any longer, ſupply the want, of their peculyarly aſſigned Territories.

Moreouer, this forſetted Prouiſion , by ſome of the ſmaller Barkes,
of the Pety-Nauy, may very ſpeedily , and with ſmall extraordinary Charges, be carryed, & landed, either in the very place, where (then) the Dearth
pincheth the Commons , moſt: or, in any other place: from whence , very commodiouſly , by farder Landiſh or Inlandiſh Carriage of it, (from
the Sea ſide , Or, from any Hauen or Creke,) it may be brought: (yea , if
nede be), into the very Hart, and Myddle of this *Albion* .

And here, it is to be Conſidered, alſo : that the Mony, ariſing of the
foreſayd

forefayd Charitable Sale, of the forfet, will, the one half thereof, become due to the Threafory of our Soueraign : And the other half, to the *Cofers of the Pety-Nauy-Royall : which is (in effe&) the Threafory of the Commons, and Common-wealth. And thus, the Priuate difordr of fome one, or a few naughty perfons, is fo prudently corre&ed, that, (befides the deferued Penalty, layd vpon the Offenders Backs : and the Publik Terror, thereby procured to the like mynded Mifers,) both the Vittailes them felues, do relieue and pleafure many Hundreds of honeft and faithfull Subie&s : And the Mony therof, alfo, is no les profitable to the encreafing of the Threafories; afwell of our moft Gracious Queene, as alfo, of the Pety-Nauy-Royall.

The Threafory of the Common-Wealth.

And, Seeing that the accuftomed Goodnes, (yea the moft mercifull and Bountifull æternall prouidence) of our heauenly Father, is fuch, appropriated vnto this Ile of *Albion*; that, by the *Fertility of the Soyle, and due Induftry of Man, employed thereto, it is very plentifully and holefomly hable (one yere, with an other, and moft commonly). to Vittayle * Two tymes fo many more, as the Naturall Subie&s of this Land are, in multitude, of Men, Women and Children, (So that, the fame, might, by very good Order, be referued within this Kingdom.) Who is there then, of any found reafon, or experience, that can dout, that the *Neceffary Vittayling of the Pety-Nauy-Royall, (The Men therof, being but a little Parcell, of the whole Body-Politik, of this Kingdom,) can caufe any vndue Want, or Dearth of vittayles?

The Fertility of this ALBION.
Note this Hypothefis.
An Argument Infoluble.

Seeing, alfo, by this *Hypothefis*, it followeth, that within euery Three yeres, fpace (Ordinarily,) Stoare may be Layd vp, for Six yeres : or, at the leaft, for Fowr : to maintayn the whole Realm: yea, though, for two yeres together, neither Wheat, nor Barly did grow at all, in the fame: or, at the moft, did yeld (clere) but fower graynes, for one, fowed.

Note.

And, where I fpeake, of Corn and Grayn referuing: I mean, no longer, Store to be made thereof, then (holefomly) the fame may * ferue. Wherein, alfo, is many a foule fault committed; in this Kingdom : either by the diuelifh Greedy gurs, ouer long keping back their Corn from the Common Market : or by other, to negligently vfing it, (in fhorter tyme) referued.

The Norimberg Secret, (or other) of Corne Referuing well, many yeres, is to be made a great account of. Vide Theop. Banofium. in Epiſt. præfixa Libello P. Rami de Religione Chriſtiana.

But, when, Extraordinary plentifull yeres do come, then, may the Publik Threafory, fele the great Extraordinary Benefit therof: (as, before is told, how:) And, alfo, the Ordinary Store, yerely be layd vp, Notwithftanding.

And, here, you may Note : that, very feldom, any Dearth, onely of God his fending, doth continue aboue two, or *three yeres, togither, continually.

Note.
Except that Vniuerfall Dearth, in Ioſeph his tyme, moft Extraordinarily, continuing Seuen Yeres together: as God had forefhewed, that it fhould. Geſ. 41.

Therefore, I Conclude, that we of this Kingdom; might (vpon wife Order taken, and inuiolably obferued,) fo enioy continuall Plenty: Or (at the leaft,) Sufficiency of all manner of moft nedefull Vittayles : (And of Corn and grayn chiefly,) that, the price of Wheat, fhould not, in any Common Market, arife * aboue a Mark the Quarter: Rye, x.s. and Barly, viij.s. the Quarter. And, So, Proportionally, of Peafon, and Beans.

F.j.   And

Note this , I pray you . For , it is One of the Chief and beſt means , to bring the Pryces of all things (eyther Naturall , or , Artificiall ,) to that Tempera-ment , which is moſt Commo-dious , both , for the Buyer , and Seller : And For the Land-lord , and Far-mer , all the Realm ooer .

And Butter , * Not aboue ij .d . the pound : and Cheſe , not aboue a peny the pound , &c . And here , I vſe this phraſe , Not aboue : For , rather , the Prices will be les . And thereupon , you may eaſily Conclude , that all Laboring Men , Handicraft Men , and other , may affoord their Labors , yea , and wares , better cheape . And ſo , a marueilous number of other Commodities , will therof enſue : wherof , any man of experience , or good iudgement , will ſone perceiue the Dependency , or Conſequency.

Vnto which peculiar great Bleſsing of God , our enioying , No certayner , readyer , and eaſier means , can be deuiſed , Than , by the Continuall Circuits of our PETY-NAVY-ROYALL : Thereby , (beſides many other Commodities , enſuing) either keping in , and terrifying the wretched harts of them , who , vndu-ly wold , (els ,) proloyn Corn , and Vittailes , out of this Realm : Or cat-ching them by the back , aſſone as they begin to Cros the Seas , to any forreyn Nation . Of which point , this may ſuffice to aduertiſe them , that are faithfully willing , to follow conſtantly the Redres , and Reforma-tion of the manifolde diſorders , herein , continually committed , againſt the Weale-Publik of this Brytiſh Monarchy .

An Anſwer to them who think that by the Pro uiſion of Vit-tails , for the Pety-Nauy-Royall , Waſt , or Spoyle of Vittayles , is made .

And , where the Quantity of Vittayles , before hand , together , at once prouided , Maketh a Shew , of great Waſte , either made , or in Danger to be made : (yf Diligent Regarde therof , be not had :) Weake Brayn hath that Man , that wold think Waſte to be made , for Laying vp together , in a Fortnights ſpace , ſo much , as ſhall not be ſpent , in Fowr-tene Wekes . But , yf there ſhould ſo much be ſpent in a Fortnight , as wold duly ſerue the Nauy Fowrtene Wekes : Then were there Waſte , in-dede : And ſo , ſome Want , fondly procured , more , than els is nedefull. Or , yf , vnder Pretence of Beof Powldring , for the Pety-Nauy-Royall , ſome Fals Iudas wold ſteale or proloyn A Hogſhed , Two , or Six , to ſend ouer Seas , to Forreyner : And that , for Priuate Lucre : or for a Farder , and Worſer Intent , &c . But , that , and ſuch like fowle Diſor-ders , will be left now , (We Hope :) or , moſt Narrowly be ſene to : As well in Beof , as Butter , Cheſe , and Bacon , &c .

And , as for Seeing to , or Sauing of the Vittayles , that they be not loſt : Ye nede not Dowt . For , yt ſtandeth them more vpon , than ſo . And , As for Exceſſiue Feeding at Sea : Who knoweth not , their Dyet to be but Reaſonable , and Sufficient ? With Hunger rather finiſhing their Meales , than with Vnweldy Carcaſſes : Ouercharged with Meat and Drink , As among vs , at home , many a Thowſand is ?

I Omyt alſo , to ſpeak of the great Ayde of Freſh Vittayles , which the Nauy may haue , ſundry Wayes , at Seas : by Diuers kynde of good Fiſh , (our Men being ſufficiently ſkilfull , now , at length , to preuent or Cure the Skyrby .) As Pylchard , Whyting , Haddock , Playce , Sole , Cunger , Herring , Burt , Thornback , Salmon , Bream , Gurnard , Mullet , Mackerell , &c . All , being (moſt commonly ,) Better , then we haue them at Land , brought to vs . Which * good Fiſh , will alſo , be a Means , of their ſpending les Fleſh , at Sea : And therefore , to Nede the les , from Land .

So that, Yf all things be Duly, and Deeply Wayed: befydes a great number of other the Principall Benefits, Redownding to this Kingdom (by the forefayd Pety-Nauy-Royall:) it is rather thought, that the ftreict Dyet, (In dede, a moderat, prefcribed, and vniform Dyet) of our Publik freends at Sea, in the forefayd Nauy employed, will be a means of very much Vittayles, and Flefh fauing: and to help toward plenty finding, on Land. For (As Englifh-mens noted Vice, or Diforder is:) Of the felf fame Men, fome, wold at their Landifh home, or in Alehoufes, and Tauernes, eat and drink, more, then Mans nature, behoofully needeth: Or els, fome wold be more fine, delicate, and coftly in their Dyet, then wifdom and difcretion wold Prefcribe them &c. So that, No dout, can here remayn, that Dearth can haue Roote, or iuft occafion, to rife, or grow in this Kingdom, of this Temperate Dyet, allowed to them at Sea: who, els, ought to haue afmuch, or wold haue coftlyer, and more, yf they had continued on Land.

And, while the Confideration of one great Ayd, and Means, for Flefh to become better Cheap, is in our hands: I think it very needfull, to geue you to vnderftand, that by the wicked Wilfulnes only, and euident fraude, of diuers Subiects of this Realm, There is, yerely, deftroyed, more than Fiue Hundred Cart-loads of good frefh Fifh, within this our Ile of ALBION. And though, then, not Meat-able, for Man, when they are fo deftroyed: yet, within fhort tyme after, they wold be. And likewife, though, not then, likely to amount, in the whole Quantity, yerely, to fo many loads: Yet, at the tyme of their being Market-able (of the Myddle * fort) they wold euidently appere, fo, to be rated: or rather, far aboue. And neither, any more Charges, nor yet any greater trauaile of Man, is to be employed, for the fame forts of Fifh hauing and enioying: both, when they wold be (as is fayd) Markat-able: And alfo, when the forefayd great haboundance of Vittayles, by them, might be enioyed: Than is, when, fo abhominably, they are deftroyed, and vtterly fpoyled.

And, that this brief, and very needfull Aduertifement, may be found the more manifeftly true, and duly geuen: You may vnderftand, That, in the Riuer of Thames only (as my Inftructor, by Worfhipfull Ientlemen, and other Men of experience, heretofore hath tryed out) moft commonly, euery yere, by the Fifhermen belonging to fome one fmall Town (or within a little Circuit about it,) there is deftroyed, aboue a Thoufand Buffhels, of the yong Fry, of diuers kindes of good Fifh: which, in due tyme of their growth, and by lawfull order, being taken, wold haue byn hable, to fatiffie Two Hundred Thoufand Men, one day: Or, Twenty Thoufand Men, ten dayes: or, Two Thoufand Men, an Hundred dayes, or, Fowr Thoufand Men Fifty, dayes. &c.

Which Account, dependeth vpon the Rating of euery kynde of Myddle Markat-able Fifh, to be (one with an other) of Ten tymes fo much

F.ij.

A little Digreffion, againft fome Mis-Vfe of the Fifhings of the Noble Riuers of Thames, and other, within this Realm.

This Phrafe, of Myddle-Sort Markat-able, is to be vnderftood, neither of them which hard and fcant are to be iudged Markat-able: Nor of the ouer growen Fifh, and in the Superlatiue Growth (as a Man might term them,) But only of them, which, moft commodioufly are Senuifable: in refpect of Profit Publik.

Note thefe Hypothefes.

much meat , as , when , they are deftroyed in fuch Small Fry , as we mean of : And alfo , that a Bufhell of fuch Markat-able Fifh , is hable to fatiffie 20 Englifh-men , One day , for their fufficient Repafte and Suftenance : (the Bread and drinke , requifite thereto , being excepted .) What is , then , (I pray you) to be rekened , of the Publik Dammage , of 500. Cart loads , of Fifh , (yerely) thus deftroyed ? How may it (reafonably) any longer , remayn vnreformed ? Which 500 , Cartload , (according to the former Rate of Myddle Markat-able Fifh ,) do amount and ryfe , of only 2400 Bufhels of Fry , yerely deftroyed .

But , yf you fuppofe to be only 30 Trink-Boats : and that euery one of the fayd 30 Trink-Boat Nets , euery day , only for 300 , dayes , in euery whole yere , deftroy , but one Bufhell of very fmall Fry : The Somme therof , doth amount to Nyne Thoufand Bufhels of Fry , fo deftroyed , yerely . Which Fry , when it fhould be Myddle Markat-able , wold be , (one with an other) of Ten tymes more Meat and Fifh , than , when , it is fo deftroyed . Therefore , the Crafts-men of the Trink-Boats , on the Thames , may , very probably , be accufed , conuicted , iudged , and condemned , as the moft abhominable yerely Deftructioners of Nynety Thoufand Bufhels of Markat-able Fifh .

And , if you abridge me , in the number of the dayes of their Labor , yerely : I will , then , charge eche of their Nets , with deftroying dayly , more , than a Bufhell of Fry : one day , with an other , euery day of their Labor . And I know (notwithftanding ,) how much , I kepe me , within my Bounds , yet : How Horrible and Intollerable , fo euer , this Fact , doth found in your eares : who haue not liftened to this matter , before now : nor know the Verity therof , yet .

Of this Nynety Thoufand Bufhels of Fifh , if you will account but euery 48 Bufhels , (which make fix Quarters ,) to be a Cart loade : the Somme will be 1875 Cart loads , of frefh Fifh : which is deftroyed , yerely , by the Trink-Nets , only : And that , in the Noble Riuer of Thames , only . Whereby , it is moft euident , that my firft Affertion , of 500 Cart Loads of frefh Fifh , deftroyed , in the whole Realm of England , is moft vndoutedly true .

So is it , now , alfo , Probable : that , in all England , by the manifold diforder , vfed about Fry and Spawn , deftroying , there is yerely Spoyled , or Hyndred , the Broode of Two Thoufand Cart Loads , of frefh Fifh , of myddle Markat-able fkantlyn .

The Publik Loss yerely caufed by the Trink-Boats , Kiddels , &c. is vncredible to them that know not the Truthe : Or , will not Search , and Examine to the quick , what Violent , or , rather Fraudulent Diforder , is therin Practifed.

The Value , of the forefayd Nynety Thoufand Bufhels , of frefh Fifh , (one with an other , being rated at fiue Shillings a Bufhell) is Two and Twenty Thoufand , and Fiue Hundred Pounds , of Current Mony of England .

Which quantity of Fifh , alfo , (according to our former Hypothefes) wold mainteyn , for one day , a Thoufand Thoufand , and Eight Hundred Thoufand Men . Or , Nyne Hundred Thoufand Men , two dayes : Or , Three Hundred Thoufand

fand Men, fix dayes: Or, a Hundred Thoufand Men, 18 dayes:
Or, Fifty Thoufand Men, 36 dayes: Or, 25 Thoufand Men,
72 dayes. &c.

And, yf, in the Riuer of Thames, Trinker-men only, do not (in your
Opinion, or, in the eftimation and knowlege of them, who are fomwhat
expert in thefe Cafes,) feme duly charged, with this Incredible Spoyle, and
Dammage Publik: I will allow, vnto you and them, into this Reckening
(to make vp, the full and heaped vp meafure, of this abhominable Iniquity) all the Deftruction of Fry, and yong Fifh, which the 18, or, 19 Tym-
ber-Nets, do yerely make: who are fayn, euery two howrs of the Flud
or Tyde, to difcharge their Nets, for feare of breaking. I will geue you
in, alfo, the Spoyle, which is yerely made with the Engynes, called
Kyddels. And they, are in the Thames, aboue an Hundred and Forty. And now, you can not dout, but I haue good reafon, to warrant
you, that the Deftruction and Spoyle of Fry and yong Fifh, made yerely, and that* only, by the Three former vnlawfull Engynes, (occupied in
the Thames) doth amount, yerely, to the forefayd Publik los, of 90000
Bufhels of Myddle Markat-able good Fifh: In the Totall Somme: I mean,
when, the fame fhould come to be, of Myddle Markat-able growth.
Though, at the tyme of their Spoyling them, they are, in Meafure, but
Nyne Thoufand Bufhels.

And, bycaufe, the 30, or 31 Trinker-Men, not *· only, are the chiefeft
Caufe, of the forefayd exceeding great Deftruction of FRY, and yong
Fifh, (to the Intollerable Dammage Publik,) but *· alfo, lye in the Riuer of Thames, to the great Annoyance, and Cumber (many tymes)
of the Ships, and Boats, paffing betwene London, and Grauefend (and
farder:) And otherwhile, to the loffe, both of Goods and Liues, of many of her Maiefties Louing, and Faythfull Subiects: What difcrete Subiect, or true Member of the Brytifh, or Englifh Monarchie, is there,
who, in his hart, Doth not abhorre this Haynous Enormity? and will not,
with his Voyce, Hartily, Cry owt, and Say: Fy on them, Fy on
them: Away with them, Away with them: Who, fo abhominably, conuert Mans Meat, to the Feeding of *· Swyne: And O-
therwhile, *· Bury fome of their vnlawfull Spoyle of Fry, and young Fifh,
in the Shores of the Thames, and Otherwhere.

God, of his infinite Goodnes, fendeth vs (Yerely) Euident To-
kens, of the great Habundance, of this kynde of good Vittailes, prepared purpofely for this parte, of this Brytifh Albion: But, thefe Tryn-
ker-Men, Caft IncredibleMuch of fuch a Threaior, before their Swyne,
to Battle them withall: And are, (by that meanes,) great Hynderers,
both to the Wealth, and Reliefe Publik: and alfo, to the Glory of God:
Who, wold be Duly Glorifyed, and Prayfed of many a Thowfand of the
Rich, and Poore, who, fhould be Serued, Pleafured, and Relieued, with
the great Habundance, of the Dyuers forts of good and wholefome Fifh,
Swarming in this Incomparable Riuer of Thames (from the

For, by many other meanes, the Fry and Spawne of Fifh is deftroyed: as Partely by the Statute made Anno 4 Henrici Septi. Cap. 15, may appear: and Partly, by our dayly Experience, may be perceyued.

Much lyke Diforders, haue heretofore byn vfed, about Orford Hauen, in the County of Suffolk. Read the Statute made Anno 4 Henrici VII. Cap. 11.

one end therof, to the other,) in very mayn Skulls: Yf thefe Publik Enemies of God and Man, did not (more than Barbaroufly, and les than Chriftianlike,) vtterly fpoyle, and wickedly tred vnder their feet, fuch a Bleffing and liberall Gift of our GOD, and moft louing heauenly father, profered vnto vs, and in manner, put into our hands.

Very much, more abhominable, and more vnreafonable, is the wickednes of thefe Trinker-men, than was the Diforder, heretofore (and till of late) committed in Ireland : where, the Inhabitants of diuers Cities and Towns, adioyning nere to Riuers, that do Eb and Flow (in which Riuers, the Fry of Salmon, Ele, and other Commodious Fifh are bred and nourifhed) did kepe great heards and numbers of Swyne : which, at low water, they do, or (till of late) did lead, or fuffer, to fede vpon the Strands, of the fayd Riuers : where they do, or did, deftroy great Quantity of Salmon, and Ele Fry : and of diuers other good Fifhes : to the great hurt, and hindrance of Fifhing : and the exceeding great dammage, of the Common-Wealth. As, by the Act, made againft the fame, at *Dublyn*, *Anno vndecimo*, of our moft Gracious Souerayn Lady, Queene Elizabeth, more at large, may appere.

And, at this prefent, I am the bolder, to expres my Inftructor his feruency, againft the Trinker-Men, their haynous endammaging of the Publik-wealth of this Kingdom : Seeing, for (abowt) an Hundred and Fifty yeres ago, the whole Body of this Realm, by their Parlement Senators, left vnto vs, worthy Record of their vigilant Eye (to finde out fuch Offences) and their Politik Prouifo : by very good Iuftice, either to Cut of the Caufe, of fo greuous hindrance to the Common-wealth : or, difcreetly to punifh the fact (fo often, as it fhould be Committed) with a Hundred Shillings, to be Forfetted, to the King.

In the Second yere, of King Henry the Sixth, thefe are the wordes of the Statute, to our purpofe, prudently eftablifhed: *CAP. XV.*

Item, it is Ordeined, that the Standing of Nets, and Engins, called *Trinks*, and all other manner of Nets, which be, and were wont to be faftened, and hanged continually, day and night, by a certayn tyme, in the yere, to great Pofts, Boats, and Anchors, ouerthwart the Riuer of *Thames*, and other Riuers of the Realm, (which Standing, is a Caufe and an Occafion of as great, [and more] deftruction of the Broode; and Fry of Fifh, and Difturbance of the Common Paffage of veffels, as be the Weares, Kyddels, or any other Engins,) be wholy defended, for *EVER*. And that, euery Perfon, that fo fetteth, or faftneth them, from henceforth, to fuch Pofts, Boats, and Anchors, or like thing, continually to Stand, (as afore is fayd,) and be duly therof, by the Cowrs of the Law, conuict: he fhall forfait to the King. C.S. at euery tyme, that he is fo proued, in Default. Prouided alwayes, that it fhall be lawfull to the Poffeffors of the fayd Trinks, (if they be of* Affife,) to Fifh with them, in all feafonable tymes : Drawing and conueying them, by Hand: as, other Fifhers, do other Netts: and not faftning, or tacking the fayd Netts, to the Pofts, Boats, and Anchors: continually to Stand, as afore is fayd. Sauing alwayes, to euery of the Kings liege People, their Right, Title, and Enheritance, in their Fifhings, in the fayd Water.

But,

But, what shall any Zealous Louer of Iustice, and good Publik Policy, say, or think, herein? Seeing, so long ago, so Iust, sufficient, and
easy a Remedy, was prouided, against these Trink-Boats: aswell, for
the manifold Cumber, Danger, and Dammage, happening by them, to
such, as should, and did pas (Vp or Down,) vpon the Thames, by
Day: and chiefly in the Dark Nights, and Foggy Weather: As also, a-
gainst the exceeding great Publik-Dammage, to the Naturall and Ordinary Encrease, of very good Fish, (of diuers sorts) wilfully, and very vngodly, procured by the sayd Trinker-men, hath byn, no better regarded?

And, seeing, " Sutes in the Law, haue byn, in our dayes, commen-
ced, and followed (by vertue of the sayd Act) against the sayd Trinker-
men: And they, therupon Condemned: And yet (that notwithstanding,)
their vnlawfull Practises, still are continued?

And Thirdly, Seeing, (before our Eyes,) the Dammage to the Common-wealth, and the incredible hinderance to that plenty of Victailes finding and enioying, which God hath prepared for vs, is, by these Trinker-
men procured, more now, than euer before, most vnlawfully, and fraudulently: *etiam, cum Calumnia quadam,* to the Pitifull Clemency, and the very
great Lenity, vsed toward them?

Therfore, Seeing, (I saye,) that Neither the foresayd very good Law,
can feare them: Nor, the Amercements, (as they are vsed,) do sufficiently pinch them: Nor, the manifold iust Complaynts (besides Costly Sutes,
made and had) against these Trinker-Men, are (yet,) of sufficient effect,
to the poore Commons, to be vsed herein, according to the Lawes of
this Realm: But that, they remayn remedyles, (yet,) and are euidently
Spoyled (yerely) of an incredible great Publik Benefit, by these Trinkerly
disordred, and vnlawfull Fishings (as before is declared:) How can I, hope,
that, vpon this very brief, and simple Aduertisement, of my Instructor,
These Trink-Nets shall vtterly, and speedily, be cut of, without any longer sinister means to be vsed, by any Subiects, to beard, check-mate, or,
to deface so commendable and needfull a Statute, as that is, which before is expressed, against the Standing of any Trink-Nets? But, yet, for
all that, such is my Confidence in the goodnes of her most excellent Maiesty: and so, assured I am, her Maiesties hart, to be fraught with pitifull
Compassion, on the Lamentable, and due Complaynts, made, of the
great and exceisiue hynderance, and dammage to her Commons and Subiects wealth and relief: And, likewise, so well, are we acquainted with
the most commendable Iustice, executed by her Maiesties most Honorable Priuy Counsaile, when duly and throughly they vnderstand the
Causes: That, (with calling these things, to my Remembrance) not only, now, my Hope is reuiued: but, also, I dare half warrant the Commons, That Trink-Net-Men, henceforward, shall be vnpartially constrayned, to vse their Trade of Fishing, only, according
to the Law: and, Not, as they (most vnlawfully and very vngodly,) to long a tyme haue done, and very abhominably
at this present, they do: Yerely destroying far more Fish, than they
send, good, seasonable, lawfull, and allowable, to the Markets. For,
the

the more parte of thofe, which they fend, are Vnfeafonable or Vnlawfull Smelts, or Whiting-Mops : Wherin, the Hebber-Boats, only, might fufficiently well, (or, with much les Publik-dammage) ferue : as the wife and expert, are well affured of it.

Of the diuers, yea the manifold * other abufes, of Fifhing : or hyndrances to the fame, in this noble Riuer of Thames, only : to difclofe, rehears, and expres the matter, and manner, particularly, fully, and vnpartially, it doth require a peculiar, and great Treatife.

But, to Conclude this neceffary Digreffion ; withall : I may, aptly enough (and omitting many other,) Note only two manners of Hyndrances : Which, (eafily, and moft quickly) may be redreffed: The one, is, of long tyme vfed, and (I know not, why,) permitted: and yet (notwithftanding) is a great Hindrance and caufe of Deftruction, to the Weftern ftore of diuers kyndes of good Fifhes. I mean, aboue London Bridge, vpward (which is Weftward.) And that is, the Fifhing with any manner of Net, in the places, which either for a Seafon, or in the other; which are continually exempted from being Fifhed in, (commonly called Seueralls, and Rough places.) In which places, what vnlawfull, or vndue Subtlety is vfed, to auoyd the Roughs, and Stakes, for feare of hurting, or renting of their Nets, (and yet, to beat, and punch the Beds, or Skulls of Fifh : and by [in manner] thundring flowncing, thumping, and pafhing, or, with Chayn drawing vnder the water, &c : to driue the Fifh, to their Nets) may eafily be vnderftood, and dayly fene, or nightly hard, and perceiued. But, with all men, of fufficient Iudgement (in many Refpects,) it may be condemned, as a great hyndrance to the Broode and Store preferuing : and a violent breaking, of the firft Intent of the Politik Ciuill Senators: who, made the Ordonances, for fuch Places Seueralling, or vtterly Exempting, and referuing vnranfakt, and vndifturbed. And though Peter-Men, will ꞌmake great fhew of good Argument, to the Contrary : yet, it is beft, to make fure woork : in Circumfpectly eftablifhing the Priuilege, and exemption of thofe peculiarly affigned, and well known places, of Store and Broode: from any manner of Net cafting in the fame, or any artificiall difturbance, purpofely, therin to be vfed, for any Fifh taking.

The Second Hyndrance, is the Stinching, Soyling, (or, rather Beflouening,) of the Thames : Both Shores, and Channels : Where, the yerely Recours, and far more Plentifull Haunt, than now is, of the Weftern * Smelt; (which is the Seafonable, and beft Smelt) was wont to be. Which kynde of Fifh, greatly abhorreth fuch Fylthy grownd. And this new, and to bold Attempt, hath, but of very late yeres, exceffiuely, bin enterprifed: Not only, (as I fayd,) to the great Hyndrance of the beft, and moft Seafonable Smelt, his annuall Delight, as in times paft (and till, of very late) to Return, and abyde in great Plenty, for the fpace of the whole Seafon, in the Ancient Place of the chief Weftern Smelt Fifhing: But, alfo, to the caufing of many lothfome Sights, horrible Sauours, and infectuous euaporations, of fuch Dunghill ftuf : to no little grief of Sent, and no les danger to the health of very many, of Court, Cuntry, and City : which, either do frequent, or (now and then) pas vpon the fame Riuer

Though all other Abufes be here Vntouched, yet, that vnlawfull Engyn, at Myll Tayles, From Stanes Weftward, (called a B V C K, Wherewith, in fome one Night a Buthell of Salmon Fry, is deftroyed :) wold Spedely, and Seuerely, be Abolifhed.

The Seafonable Repayr, of the Weftern Smelt, is a matter of great Importance: Both, for the very wholefome, and Plentifull Vittayling of Multitudes of all States: And alfo, for the good help, of many a poore Fifherman, toward his Maintenance, (for that Seafon:) Both for Meat, and Mony, for him, and his Family.

Riuer of Thames, betwene the City of London, and Richemond : where (moſt vſually) our Soueraygn , euery yere , doth make ſome abode.

Betwene which two places , as our Soueraigns , (Kings and Queenes) haue very often , and (almoſt) yerely , heretofore , paſſed by water : So , durſt no man , in thoſe dayes , ſo careleſly , and vnlawfully annoy , and be-ſtinche the Thames : either , Banks or Shores , (in that Tract of the Ri-uer , chiefly : being , alſo , the fayreſt and pleaſanteſt paſſage , of the whole Riuer :) both , in reſpect of not offending , either the Eye , or Smell , of the Maieſty Royall : and alſo , for feare of breaking * Ordonances , gene-rally prouided , and very duly appliable to the ſame Caſe.

---

* The Statute.

THat No Perſon , or Perſons , after the firſt day of Au-guſt , next comming , do caſt , or vnlade , out of any man-ner of Ship , Crayer , or any other veſſell , (being within any Hauen , Rode , Channell or Riuer , flowing or running to any Port-Town , or to any Citie , Borough , or Town , with in this Realm , or any other the Kings Dominions , any manner of Balaſt , Rubbiſh , Grauell , or any other wrack , or Filth , but only vpon the Land , aboue the Full Sea Mark : Vpon Payn , that euery Perſon and Perſons , offending this Act , to loſe and forfait , for euery tyme ſo offending , *Fiue Pounds : the one half to the King our Soueraign Lord , and the other half therof , to ſuch Perſon and Perſons , as will ſue for the ſame , by Byll , Playnt , O-riginall writ or Information , in any the Kings Courts of Record , in which Action , or Sute , no wager of Law ſhalbe admitted , nor any Eſſoyne or Protection allowed. Anno 34. Henrici . 8. Cap . 9.

* The Statute againſt Annoyance , and Infection by Dung. &c.

ITem for that ſo much Dung and Filth of the yſſues and Intrals aſwell of Beaſts killed as of other Corruptions , be caſt and put in Dyches , Riuers , and other waters , and alſo within many other places , within , about , and nigh vnto diuers Cities , Boroughs and Towns of the Realm , and the Suburbs of them , that the Ayre , there , is greatly corrupt and infect : and many Maladies & other intolerable Diſeaſes do dayly happen , as well to the Inhabitants , and alſo Dwellers in the ſayd Cities , Boroughs , Towns , and Suburbs , as to o-ther , thither repayring , and paſſing , to the great An-noyance , Domage and Perill of the Inhabitants , Dwel-lers , Repayrers and Paſſers aforeſayd . It is accorded and aſſented , &c. Anno. xij . Richardi Secundi . Cap . xiij.

And how , either already , it hath of-fended , or may here after , offend the Eye and Noſe , and be dan gerous to the health ; aſwell of the right Honourable , Priuy Counſailers to our Soueraygn , or , of o-ther of the Nobility : or , of the Ladyes and Ientlewemen of the Court : As of ve-ry many other alſo , of all Degrees : any man may eaſily iudge , that either hath thoſe his two * Senſes 1. ſound and perfect : or good vnderſtanding of * Decorum obſer- 2. uing , in reſpect of Cleanlynes and whol ſomnes in Publik and Princely Paſſages : or who hath due and expert * perceiue- 3. rance , that , both it is Vnlawfull , and al-ſo Needles , in Such Maner to be done , as it is ?

And ſome , haue of late , ſo much en-croached vpon the Patience of the Commons (in this vndecent and vnlawfull filthy Attempt :) yea , ſo far , as , not only , by Scattrings , they haue annoyed the Chan-nels ,

nels, and Publik Shoares , with the fayd Dung : and (in fome places , nere the vfuall Landing of the right honorable Priuy Counfaile , and Embaffadors : and of other her Maiefties Subiects , of all forts) with the often Recours of the Carts to the Dung-boats fides , haue made fuch Publik Shores , and Stronds , as before , were very clean , hard , and grauelly, to become (thereby) very myry , and depe to the knees : and vyly ftinking , at the Eb, when the Sunne hath had any power thereon : And chiefly , if the wynde do cary the Noyfome Sauour therof , toward any man : But * alfo haue made two kynde of Standing-Leyftoofs or Dung-hils : the one immediatly to receiue from Boat the forefayd Filth : And the other , not far of : and nere , or in the High and Publik wayes : or in the Lords wafte adioyning. Both which kyndes of new deuifed Dung-hills , if heretofore , any Law or Policy did permit , or rather, not fufficiently preuent : yet (notwithftanding that flight permiffion , or want of *Prouifo* : better Confideration , aduife , and examining of the matter , will or may finde good Remedy for the noyfome Diforder : and eftablifh fome fufficient * Order : afwell , for apt places affigning , or admitting , for certayn Leyftoofs making : as alfo , for a very fhort tyme limiting for fuch ftuf , lying or continuing there , to the great Annoyance , and poffible Infection , not onely and chiefly of the nere Inhabitants , but of them alfo , which do and fhall pas thereby : of what Dignity , Degree , or State fo euer , they (he or fhe) are : Englifh , or Forreiner.

And , though the Hufband-Men , therabout , do greatly allow fuch kynde of helping their poore and hungry erable groundes : more , now , than in tymes paft : yet , this Notable dangerous , and needles annoying of fo many Thoufands , of the Queenes Maiefties louing Subiects : (and that for a very few Hufband-mens fanfies) hath not holpen them , to be hable, or (at the leaft) admonifhed them , to be the more willing , to fell their Corn any better cheap , either at Market , or at Home , to their poore Neighbours , or , to other . And yet (forfothe) for their onely Priuate wealth amending, they dare be fo bold , or are become fo careles , to annoy , and vnlawfully to vex , with lothefome Sights , and vnwholfome Sauours , fo many , and fo much , as they do . Yea , and that , dayly : and more and more . Farder I will not (as now) fay , in this vnpleafant matter : though I could.

But , in this point , (as in many other ,) the poore Commons , and quiet Subiects of her Maieftie , do Hope , that fome Redres , will fpeedily enfue . So , that Priuate Gayn, Delight, or wilfulnes , fhall not fo much either rechlefly , craftily , or violently , deuoure , or bar the PROFIT-PVBLIK : or , be fo Noyfom, and greeuous, to the poore Commons : Whofe Health and welfare , ought , in all good Common-Wealths , to be carefully procured , and conftantly maynteined : as much , as any Humayn , or their beft Policy , can aduaunce, and preferue the fame.

The Third and laft Dowt, is of the Due, True, and Iuft, Beftowing , of fuch a Maffe of Threafor , which yerely will be , Ordinarily, Contributed : and odly , otherwife , now and then : as by Gift while men are lyuing : Or, by Legacy, after their Deceafe : and fundry other-

otherwayes . The meaning hereof, is this: That the Threasor Contributed, may fundry wayes be abuſed. As, Partly, through the corrupt Nature, and very falſhood of ſuch, as ſhould in Office haue the fingring of
yt; Being not contented with their ſufficient Salary, and Due Allowance.
Or, by Vndiſcrete beſtowing ſome parte thereof: by waſting it to other
purpoſes, or vſes, than it is meant, intended, and contributed for: one tyme
or other . Or, by fayned Robberyes: or Los, by Negligent Wayes. Or
(perhaps) the Poore Commons, and Body of the Realm, may (to
Scrupulouſly) ſettle in their Fanſyes, A Speciall Dowt herein, which
they dare not expreſſely Declare: As might be, To conſider many things,
which haue bene, in tymes paſt, Liberally geuen to vſes Publik, and to
Gods great Honor: (As, in thoſe Dayes, Chriſtian Religion, was rated.)
And the ſame Gifts, then, moſt circumſpectly alſo, by the beſt Aduiſe
of Lawyers, (in Tenor of woords) ordred: And with many other Circumſtances, confirmed : Yet, Notwithſtanding all that Aſſurance, And
the Force of Legacy Law: Many a Thouſand Pounds Rent, of ſuch Free
Gifts, haue byn in our Dayes, by Act of Parlement, turned from the
firſt appoynted Vſes: And Therefore, herein alſo, mought the lyke Alteration be Dowted.

¶Eaſily, and Probably, their Fantazies might, in this their
Dowt, be ſatiſſied . Firſt, the Caſes are very vnlike . For, there, either
withowt Aduiſe and Conſent of the whole State: Or, of a Simple Intent, but Vaynly, (in Reſpect of the Means, to obtayn that their Intent,) ſuch
Gifts were Firſt geuen : But, in this our Gift, and Publik Oblation, the
whole Realm is priuy : the whole Realm conſenting: the whole Realm, ayding : And the whole Realm, certainly feeling the Publik Commodity of
Peace, Wealth, and of Bleſſed Security, thereby, enioyed . And,
Seeing the Caſe ſo ſtandeth, who can Dout, that euer hereafter, in any
Parlement, all the Parlement Senators, or the more parte, will be ſo
much corrupted in their Iudgements : as, either to miſlike the Continuall Garde of this Monarchy, by the foreſayd Pety-Nauy-Royall: or, to
Sollicite it to be layd aſide, in parte, or in all : And wold (notwithſtanding) haue the Commons, and Realm, vrged to the Contynuance of the foreſayd Perpetuall Beneuolence : for Sea Security onely, meant, and giuen ?

¶Secondly, to Preuent the likelyhood or poſſibility of ſuch dangerous Innouations : No les Wiſdom and Prudency, may herein be vſed,
than was in *Athenes*, vpon Occaſion, not vtterly vnlike to this : But, ours,
for manifold Purpoſes, to vs, more Commodious, than theirs, could be
to them.

The *Peloponneſians*, being returned homeward from *Attica*, *Thucidides*
Lib. 2) recordeth ſome of the *Athenienſiens* new Ordonances enſuing : Saying:

*Poſt quorum diſceſſum, Athenſenſes Praſidia & excubias diſpoſuerunt, in
Terra, & in Mari, ſicut volebant per totum Belli tempus ſeruari . Et decreue-
runt * Mille Talenta de Pecunia in Arce poſita, à reliqua ſumma ſegregata, ſepara-
tim reponenda eſſe, neq, inſumenda : ſed de Reliqua Pecunia, in Bello ſumptus fa-*
G.ij. *ciendos.*

An Anſwer to
this Dowt of
the Commons.

1.

2.

Which is, very
nere, Six Hun-
dred Thouſand
FRENCH
Crownes: and
vnderſtanding
thoſe Talents to
be of Siluer:
So, will one
French Crown
be Rated at 10
Drachms, Ar-
ticall in Siluer.

ciendos . Si quis ſuaderet , vel decerneret , vt ea Pecunia moueretur , aut in alios Vſus expenderetur , quàm cùm Hoſtes Atticam Claſſe & Nauali Exercitu peterent , & reprimendi eſſent , Illi Suaſori , Pœnam ſtatuebant SVPPLI-CIVM CAPITIS . Et centum Triremes præcipuas atq̃ inſtructiſſimas , quotannis , à reliqua Claſſe ſeiunxerant , adiunctis ſingularum Præfectis : Quibus , vnà cum Pecunia illa , ad nullam rem vti fas erat , præterquam , cùm Ciuitas , illa extrema neceſsitate & Periculo premeretur . The like *Promiſo* , hath byn in ſundry other Realms , eſtabliſhed : And in this Kingdom alſo , ordeyned : And , in this Caſe , full well , and neceſſarily , may be.

3.   ¶And , here alſo , ſuch other Circumſpect Conſiderations of *Promiſo* , will vndoutedly be had , againſt all fals and negligent Officers , in any Seruice Publik , (to the vſe and behoof , of the foreſayd Pety-Nauy-Royall , appointèd :) That , ſo ſone , as , any of them , ſhall be ſufficiently conuicted of falſhood , in their Office , vſed : Rigorous and ſharp Iudgement (according to the greatnes of the fault ,) ſhall pas againſt them : and they vtterly be diſhabled for euer , From all Publik function of Office , within the Realm of England , and Ireland : vpon a Band of Recogniſance , taken of their hands , to that Intent . And the matter , Proces and Concluſion , fully to be Recorded , in two books : with the Offenders Name , ſubſcribed with his own hand : (As , ſundry other things , els , are , for Safety , and Readynes , to be twiſe , or oftner Regiſtred .) And if any Officer ſhall , twiſe , or thriſe , be found a Treſpaſer , by his own Negligence , or of any vnder him : in any matter of Importance , touching his Office : After due Amends ſhall by him , or his Sueries , be made , to the Publik Threaſory : That Negligent Officer , ſhall be put out of his Office , immediatly . And , after this , or ſome better Rate , all Faults , and Offences of Falſhood , and Negligences , and ſuch like , in euery kinde of Officers (to the Pety-Nauy-Royall belonging ,) ſhall diligently (by apt Surueyors) be ſene to , and quikly eſpyed : narrowly ſifted , and duly correc-ted . So that (vndoutedly) ſuch Iuſtice , being vnpartially , and ſpeedily vſed , ſhall make , that , ere long , all theſe Officers , from the loweſt to the Higheſt , ſhall be tryed , approued , graue , honeſt , diſcrete , and circumſpect Men : who will deale ſo iuſtly , carefully , and diligently , as their Othes receiued , ſhall bynde them : And their ſufficient Sueries , ſhall be anſwearable for : And , as , the whole Commons will hartily requeſt them , for to do : and will , moſt faithfully promiſe vnto them , and gladly performe (vpon their good ſeruice , and due deſert) ſuch extraordinary Rewards , and ſo great , as may encourage any Chriſten Man , to deale truly , and iuſtly , in ſo waighty Affaires Publik : And may alſo reioyce any godly mans hart els , to ſee excellent Vertue , receiue ſuch Publik Honor , Credit , and Gwerdon.

4.   ¶To Conclude : who Douteth , but that our King and God , of his Infinite mercy may graunt vs , euen at our firſt diſcrete and circumſpect Choys , and aſſigning , to finde all ſorts of thoſe Officers , ſo wiſe , faithfull , Iuſt , Carefull , and Diligent : as , it may be accounted his very handy-work , and great Bleſſing , herein ? Whoſe Mercifull Prouidence , at no tyme , is wanting in matters Coſmopoliticall , of great importance : and
which ,

which , alſo , incomparably ſurpaſſeth all Humayn Policie : though the ſame be moſt carefully vſed, for matters tending greatly and chiefly to his Glorie, and Honor : as , vndoutedly , this doth . And ſo , are the Three former Douts, briefly, and ſufficiently (as this place may admit) Diſſolued, and taken away .

Therfore, Seeing No Dout, or Obiection, (worthy of Conſideration, or, of any Importance,) is remayning, to the Contrary of that moſt zealous *WISH*, or rather , *SVPPLICATION* , which (certainly) is agreable to the Harty Deſire, of the moſt parte of all Naturall, and Faithfull Subiects of this Kingdom , at this very Preſent : (vpon our own State, both, in it ſelf, chiefly, and abſolutely : And alſo ; in Reſpect of our Forrein Neighbors , their vnaſſured Frendſhip, being Conſidered) : Why ſhould not we *HOPE* , that ; *RES-PVBL . BRYTANICA*, on her knees , very Humbly , and erneſtly Soliciting the moſt Excellent Royall Maieſty , of our *ELIZABETH*, (Sitting at the *HELM* of this Imperiall Monarchy : or , rather , at the Helm of the *IMPERIALL SHIP*, of the moſt parte of Chriſtendome : if ſo , it be her Graces Pleaſure) ſhall obteyn, (or Perfect Policie, may perſwade her Highnes,) that, which is the Pyth, or Intent of *RES-PVBL. BRYTANICA*, Her Supplication ? Which is , That, ΣΤΟΛΟΣ ΕΞΩΠΛΙΣΜΕΝΟΣ, may helpe vs ; not onely, to ✚ΠΟΥΡΙΟΝ ΤΗΣ ΑΣΦΑΛΕΙΑΣ : But make vs, alſo , Partakers of Publik Commodities Innumerable, and (as yet) Incredible. Vnto which , the *HEAVENLY KING*, for theſe many yeres laſt paſt, hath , by *MANIFEST OCCASION*, moſt Graciouſly, not only inuited vs : but alſo , hath made, *EVEN NOW*, the Way and Means, moſt euident, eaſie , and Compendious : In-aſmuch as ; (beſides all our own ſufficient Furniture , Hability , Induſtry , Skill, and Courage) our Freends are become ſtrong : and our Enemies , ſufficiently weake , and nothing Royally furniſhed , or of Hability , for Open Violence Vſing : Though their accuſtomed Confidence , in Treaſon, Trechery, and Diſloyall Dealings, be very great. Wherin, we beſeche our *HEAVENLY PROTECTOR*, with his *GOOD ANGELL* to Garde vs , with *SHIELD AND SWORD*, now , and euer . Amen .

.

G.iij.   Truly

Ruly , I can not here let pas , an other Little Difcourfe , (as there are Diuerfe ,) of his , much to this Intent . I am not vtterly Ignorant , (Sayd he ,) of the Humors , and Inclinations , of the People of this *ALBION* , being (now) the greater Portion , of the *BRYTISH IMPIRE* . For , although , as well through fo many Conquefts , as alfo , great Refortings hither , of fundry other Nations , there hath byn made a Marueilous Mixture of People , of Repugnant Conditions : Yet , from Yere to Yere , the Generall Difpofition , of the prefent Inhabitants , doth , much alike , Alter to this great Imperfection : That is : Though otherwhiles , they know and Tafte of the Beft : yet , feldome tyme , they do Conftantly follow , and continue in the fame : I mean now , in Publik Behauiour , *Et officijs Ciuilibus* : For that , their Ciuile Conuerfation , and Induftry , in many poynts , is nothing fo anfwerable to the Dignity of Man , As the very Heathens did prefcribe Rules for the Gouernment therof . Let *CICERO* , his Golden Book , *DE OF-FICIIS* , be the Euidence againft them , to the Contrary : And that , in thofe Poynts , by the Heathen Orator expreffed , which both greatly are agreable to the moft Sacred Diuine Oracles , of our *IEOVA* : and alfo , for the Common-Wealths Profperity , right Excellent.

I haue oftentymes , (Sayd He ,) and many wayes , looked into the State of Earthly Kingdoms , Generally , the whole World ouer : (as far , as it may , yet , be known to Chriften Men , Commonly :) being a Study , of no great Difficulty : But , rather , a purpofe , fomewhat anfwerable , to a perfect Cofmographer : to fynde hym felf , *Cofmopolites* : A Citizen , and Member , of the whole and only one Myfticall City Vniuerfall : And fo , confequently , to meditate of the Cofmopoliticall Gouernment therof , vnder the King Almighty : paffing on , very fwiftly , toward the moft Dreadfull , and moft Cumfortable Term prefixed :

And I finde (fayd he) that if this *Brytifh Monarchy , wold heretofore , haue followed the Aduantages , which they haue had , onward , They mought , very well , ere this , haue furpaffed (By Iuftice and Godly , fort) any particular Monarchy , els , that euer was on Earth , fince Mans Creation . And that , to all fuch purpofes , as to God are moft acceptable : And to all perfect Common-Wealths , moft Honorable , Profitable , and Comfortable .

But , yet , (fayd he) there is a Little lock of *LADY OCCA-SION* , Flickring in the Ayre , by our hands , to catch hold on : wherby , we may , yet ones more (before , all , be vtterly paft , and for euer) difcretely,

Cofmopolites

The Brytifh Monarchy hath byn Capable of the greateft Ciuile Felicity , that euer was any Particular Monarchy , Els , in the whole world : Yea , fo Incomparably , that it might haue Cõtended , for the Generall Monarchie.

difcretely , and valiantly recouer , and enioy , if not all our Ancient and due Appertenances , to this Imperiall Brytifh Monarchy , Yet , at the leaft , fome fuch Notable Portion therof , As , (all Circumftances , duly and Iuftly appertayning to Peace and Amity , with Forreyn Princes , being offred and vfed) this , may become the moft Peaceable , moft Rich , moft Puiffant , and moft Florifhing Monarchy of all els (this day) in Chriftendome . Peaceable (I fay) euen with the moft parte of the felf fame Refpects , that good King Edgar had , (being , but a Saxon :) And by fundry fuch means , as , he chiefly , in this Impire did put in proof and vre , Triumphantly . Wherupon , his Surname , was *PA-CIFICVS* , moft aptly and Iuftly . This Peaceable king Edgar , had in his mynde (about 600 . yeres paft) the Reprefentation of a great parte of the felf fame *Idea* , which (from aboue onely , and by no Mans aduife ,) hath gratioufly ftreamed down into my Imagination : being (as it becommeth me , a Subiect) Carefull for the Godly Profperity of this Brytifh Impire , vnder our moft Peaceable Queene Elizabeth .

For , *EADGARVS PACIFICVS , Regni fui profpiciens Vtilitati , pariter & Quieti , Quatuor Millia* * *Octingentas fibi Robuftas congregauit Naues : E quibus , Mille Ducentas , in Plaga Anglia Orientali : Mille Ducentas , in Occidentali : Mille Ducentas , in Auftrali : Mille Ducentas in Septentrionali Pelago* * *Conftituit : Vt ad Defenfionem Regni fui , contra Exteras Nationes , bellorum Difcrimina fuftinerent :*

O wifdom Imperiall : moft diligently , to be Imitated . *Videlicet , PROSPICERE* : to Forefee : O Charitable Kingly Parent , that was touched with Ardent Zeale , for Procuring the Publik-Profit of his Kingdom : Yea and alfo , the Peaceable enioying therof . O , of an Incredible Maffe of Threafor , a Kingly Portion , yet , in his Cofers , remayning : Yf , then , he had , (or late before ,) any warres : Seeing no Notable Tax , or Contribution Publik , is (Hiftorically) mentioned , to haue byn , for the Charges hereof , leuyed . Yf , in Peace , he him felf , florifhed fo wealthyly . O marueilous Politicall and Princely Prudency , in tyme of Peace , to Forefee and preuent , (and that , moft Puiffantly and Inuincibly) all poffible malice , fraude , force , and mifchief Forreyn . O moft difcrete Liberality , to fuch excellent good vfes , powring out his Threafor , fo abundantly . O faithfull Englifh People (Then) and Worthy Subiects , of fuch an Imperiall and Godly Gouernour . O your True and willing Harts , and bleffed ready hands (Then .) So , to Impart fuch Abundance of Vittayles , for thofe Huge Nauies mayntenance . So , (I fay) as , neither Dearth or Famine , feemed (fondly) to be feared of you , for any intolerable want , likely to enfue , thereby . Nor , prices of Vittayles , complayned of , to be vnreafonably enhanfed , by you : finding , for their great Sales , fo good and rare Oportunity .

with any that hath byn : If requifite Policy therto , had byn vfed in Due tyme , and Conftantly Followed .

Yf Ariftotle did Aptly fay thus of the Iland of Crete : *Videtur hac Infula ad Principatum Gracianata , at praclare Sita* (*Polit . Lib . 2 Cap. 8.*) much more Aptly , may we , Or might we haue fayd it , in refpect of all our Oppofit Neyghbors and farder of , alfo .

*
FLORES HISTOR : Radulfus Ceftrenfis hath 4000 only . Confider the probable Agreement of thefe Two Places , afterward , in the Margent . And of thefe Two words there , *STATVIT ,* and *CIR-CVMNA-VIGAVIT .* And to that *STATVIT ,* doth this word *CONSTI-TVIT* fomwhat anfwere .

This Peaceable KING EDGAR, was one of the perfect Imperiall Monarchs of this Brytifh Impire: and therfore , thus , his Fame remayneth (for euer) Recorded:

ANGLICI ORBIS BASILEVS,
FLOS , ET DECVS ÆDGARVS,
non minus Memorabilis Anglis quàm Cyrus Perfis : Romu-
lus Romanis : Alexander Macedonibus : Arfaces Parthis :
* Carolus Francis : Anno vitæ 37.ᵐᵉ Regni fui , cum
Fratre , & póft , 21.ᵐᵉ Jdibus Julij , obijt : &
apud GLASCON . Sepelitur.

And why not , ARTHVRS BRYTANLD Bycaufe king ARTHVR his Name Sene, was a Thorne in the Saxons eyes, of thofe Dayes: and his Name reherfed, was Odible to their Eares: Whofe Anceftors were by that Brytifh Arthur, 12 times , ouer-come in Bartaile.

* *Charta Regia Henrici Sec .*

Radulphus Ceftrenf .

* *Now* STATVIT. and CIRCVMNA-VIGAVIT: which declareth two orders of Ships: and fo may the Totall Summe of alfo be alfo true. He Sayling with his NAVY-ROYALL, dubble to any one of the other 4 Stationary Pety Nauyes . For MATHEVS WESTMONAS-TER, fayth 1 4800 fhe Reqular Congreffion Naues . So that he did gether fo many! And alfo affirmeth the Partitions into 4 equal Parts : And nameth their Stations : as other , doe otherwife fpeake , of the Senfible Alteration of their Stations. So that not with the other Conferred , and imperfect coniecture of the Writers being Somwhat holpen , the Verity feemeth now to be touched.

O Glaftonbury, Glaftonbury : the Threafory of the Carcaffes of fo famous , and fo many rare Perfons, (* *Quæ olim* MATER SANC-TORVM *dictaes* : & , *ab alijs ,* TVMVLVS SANCTORVM: *quæm, ab ipfis* DISCIPVLIS DOMINI , *ædificatam fuiffe , Venerabilis habet An-tiquorum Authoritas* .) How Lamentable , is thy cafe , now ? How hath Hypocrifie and Pride , wrought thy Defolation ? Though I omit (here) the names of very many other , both excellent holy Men , and Mighty Princes (whofe Carcaffes are committed to thy Cuftody,) yet , that A-poftlelike Iofeph , That Triumphant BRYTISH ARTHVR , And now , this Peaceable , and Prouident Saxon, King Edgar, do force me, with a certayn forrowfull Reuerence , here , to Celebrate thy Memory.

This Peaceable King Edgar, (as by Ancient Records may ap-pere:) His Sommer Progreffes , and Yerely chief paftymes, were, The Sayling rownd about this Whole Ile of Albion : Garded with hys Grand Nauy of 4000 Sayle, at the leaft : parted into 4 Equall Partes , of Pety Nauies : eche , being of a Thowfand Ships . For, fo it is Anciently Recorded. *Idem quoq,* ÆDGARVS, 4000 NAVES CON-GREGAVIT: *ex quibus, omni Anno, poft feftum Pafchale* 1000 *Naues aa quæmlibet Angliæ partem* * *Statuit : Sic, Æftate Infulam* * *Circumnauigauit* . Hy-*eme verò , Iudicia in Prouincia exercuit . Et hæc omnia , ad fui Exercitium , & ad Hoftium fecit Terrorem.*

Could, and would that Peaceable, and wife King Edgar, before néde (as being in Peace, and Quiet, with all Nations , about hym) And Not-withftanding , miftrufting his poffible Enemies , make his Paftymes, fo Roy-ally, Politically, and Triumphantly: with fo many Thowfand Ships : And at the leaft, with ten tymes fo many Men, as Ships : And that, yerely ? And fhall we, being not affured of fuch Neighbours frendefhips , as may

become

become, to vs, as Cruell and Tyrannicall Enemyes, as neuer King Edgar neded to Dread any the like : And they, as many, and Mighty Princes, as neuer King Edgar coped with the like ? Shall we (fayd he,) not Iudge it, some parte of Wisdome, to Imitate carefully, in some little Proportion, (though not with so many Thousands,) the prosperous Pastimes of Peaceable King Edgar, that Saxonicall Alexander? Yea, Prosperous pastimes, those may be iustly cownted, by which, he also made euident to the whole world, that, As he wisely knew the Ancient Bownds, and Limits, of this Brytish Impire : So, that he coüld, and wold, Royally, Iustly, and Triumphantly * Enioy the same: Spite of the Diuell, and Maugre the Force of any Forreyn Potentate: And, all that, so Highly, and Faithfully, to the glory of God, finally, intended, and brought to pas : As the Wisest, and Godlyest Prelats, and Cownsailors of those Dayes, (so cownted of, and recorded,) could best aduise or direct him : Or (Perchance,) but sincerely Commend, and Dutifully encourage him, in : He being, of himself, so bent : As, purposing, first, Inuincibly to Fortify the Chiefest and Vttermost Walls of his Ilandish Monarchy, against all Forreyn Encombrance possible : And in that Fortification Furdering, and Assuring, to trust best his own Ouersight, and Iudgement : in yerely vewing the same, in euery Quarter therof: And that, (as it were) for his Pastime Imperiall, also, in the Sommer Tyme : to the ende, that afterward, In all Securitie, he might, in Winter tyme * (*VACARE:*) be at conuenient Leysure, On Land : chiefly, to set furth Gods Due Honor : And Secondly, to Vnderstand, and Diligently to Listen to the Causes and Complaynts, of his Commons. For, (As *Mathæus Westmonastariensis*, of him, to his Immortall Commendation, hath left vs a Remembrance:)

*Habebat autem * prætereà Consuetudinem, per omnes Regni Prouincias transire : Vt intelligeret, quomodo Legum Iura, & suorum Statuta Decretorum, à Principibus obseruarentur : Et, ne Pauperes à Potentibus præiudicium passi, opprimerentur, diligenter inuestigare Solebat. In * vno, FORTITVDINI; In altero, IVSTITIÆ studens : Et Reipub. Regniq, Vtilitati consulens, in Vtroq. Hinc, HOSTIBVS circumquaq TIMOR, Et AMOR omnium erga eum excreuerat SVBDITORVM.*

Thus, we see, how, in * Opportunity, this Peaceable Edgar, procured, to this Impire, such prosperous Security : That his true and faithfull Subiects, all manner of wayes, (that is, at home, and also at Sea, both outward and inward,) mought peaceably, Safely, and Securely, employ their wits and trauayles, for the marueilous enriching of this Kingdom, and pleasuring very many other : Carrying forth, the Naturall Commodities of this Land, abounding here, aboue our necessary vses : (and due Store reserued) : And likewise (agayn), Furnishing the same, with all necessary (and not superfluous) Forreyn Commodities : set from far, or Forreyn Cuntryes. This, was, in dede (as before is Recorded) a Kingly Prouidence: *Reipub. Regniq, Vtilitati Consulens, &c.*

H.L.   Besides

Befides which great Vtility and Profit publik , forefene : and by this means , enioyed : he him felf , vfed moft gladly the Aduantage of that Security , in miniftring of Iuftice : Or caufing the fame to be executed , all his Kingdom ouer : Not Squeymifhly , frowningly , or fkornfully fhunning the ragged and tattered fleue of any * Suppliant , holding vp to him a fimple foyled Bill of Complaynt , or Petition , and that , homely contriued : Or , afrayd at , and Timeroufly hafting from , the fickly Pale face , or feeble Lymmed Suter , extremely conftrayned , fo , to fpeak for him felf : Nor , partially fmoothering his own Confcience , to fauor , or mayntein the fowle fault , and trefpas vnlawfull , of any his Subiects: How Mighty , or Neceffary fo euer , they (els) were : But , diligently made Search , leaft , *Pauperes , à Potentibus praiudicium paſſi , opprimerentur* .

☞   Thus , did Publik-"Security , from Forreyn foe , abrode : And True " loue , of his own Subiects , garding him , at home : And the " Heauenly Spirite , directing all his godly Purpofes : Caufe Iuftice and Equity , in all Quarters of this *ALBION* , to florifh . For which , his Peaceable and profperous Benefits , at the Eternall King his hand , obtayned : he became , not Infolent , or declyned to Tyrannicall Regiment (as fome Princes , in other Cuntries haue made their lyues , *Comicotragicall* ,) But with all his forefayd Inuincible Sea Strength , aboundant Wealth , Triumphant Peace : with Security , and Iuftice , ouer all his Monarchy preuayling : his hart , was continually , and moft zealoufly bent , to fet forth the Glory , Laude , and Honor of the Almighty Creator , the Heauenly and euerlafting King : By fuch principall and Princely means , as , (then ,) were demed , to God , moft acceptable: And fuch , as many Monuments , yet , to our dayes , remayning , do of him vndoutedly Teftify : As this , for one :

*ALTITONANTIS Dei largiflua Clementia , qui eſt Rex Regum , Ego ÆDGARVS Anglorum Baſileus , omniumą, Regum Inſularum , OCEANIꝢVE * BRITANNIANI Circumiacentis , Cunctarumą, Nationum quæ infra eam includuntur IMPERATOR & Dominus , gratias ago ipſi Deo Omnipotenti , Regi meo , qui meum IMPERIVM ſic ampliauit & exaltauit ſuper Regnum Patrum meorum : Qui , licet Monarchiam totius Angliæ adepti ſint , à tempore ATHELSTANI , (qui primus Regnum Anglorum , & omnes Nationes quæ Britanniam incolunt , ſibi Armis ſubegit ,) Nullus tamen eorum , vltra eius Fines , Imperium ſuum dilatare aggreſſus eſt . Mihi autem conceſſit Propitia Diuinitas , cum Anglorum IMPERIO , omnia Regna Inſularum OCEANI , cum ſuis ferociſſimis Regibus , vſq̃ NORVEGIAM : maximamq̃, Partem Hiberniæ , cum ſua Nobiliſſima Ciuitate Dublinia , Anglorum Regno ſubiugare . Quos etiam omnes , meis Imperijs colla ſubdere (Dei fauente gratia) coegi . Quapropter , & Ego , CHRISTI Gloriam & Laudem exaltare , & eius Seruitium amplificare deuotus , diſpoſui : & per meos fideles Fautores , Dunſtanum videlicet Archiepiſcopum , Æthelwoldum , & Oſwaldum Epiſcopos , (quos mihi Patres Spirituales , & Conſiliatores elegi) magna ex parte , ſecundùm quod diſpoſui , effeci . &c.*

And

And agayn, this, in an other Monument.

A. Omnipotentis Dei &c. Ipsius Nutu & gratia suffultus, Ego ÆDGARVS, Basileus Dilectæ Insulæ ALBIONIS, subditis nobis sceptris Scottorum, Cumbrorum, ac Brytonum, & omnium circumcirca Regionum, quieta Pace perfruens: *studiosius sollicitè de laudibus Creatoris omnium occupor addendis: Ne nunc Inertia, nostrisq, diebus (plus æquo) seruitus eius tepescere videatur. &c. Octauo* decimo mei Terreni IMPERII *Anno &c. Anno Incarnationis Dominicæ. 973.*

'Ego ÆDGARVS, totius ALBIONIS Basileus, hoc Priuilegium (tanta roboratum Authoritate) Crucis Thaumate Confirmaui. &c.

So that, by all these Rehearsed Records, it is most euident, that the Peaceable King Edgar, was one of those Monarchs, in whose hands (if life had sufficed,) the * Incredible Value and Priuilege, graunted by God and Nature, vnto this Brytish Monarchy, might haue byn peaceably purchased: In such sort, as the very Blessing and fauour of the Diuine Trinity, hath layd means, for our Industry to Attayn to, and enioye the same, by.

And though sundry other valiant Princes, and Kings of this Land, I could recite, which, in tymes past, haue either by Intent gone about: or, by wise and valyant exployt, haue meetly well prospered, toward this Ilandish appropriat Supremacy atteyning: Yet, Neuer, any other reasonable Means was vsed, or by Humayn wyt, and Industry, can be contriued, to all purposes Sufficient, But onely, by our SEA-FORCES preuayling: And so, by our Inuincible enioying All, within the SEA-LIMITS, of our Brytish Royallty, Conteyned.

To which Incredible Politicall Mystery atteyning, No easyer, readyer, or perfecter Plat and Introduction, is (as yet) come to my Imagination, than is, The Present and Continuall Seruice, of Threescore, good, and Tall, warlik Ships, with Twenty smaller Barks: and those 80, Ships (great and small) with 6660 apt Men, furnished: and all, singularly well appointed, for Seruice, (both on Sea and Land) faithfully and diligently, to be done, in such Circumspect and Discrete Order, As, partly, I haue in other places declared: and farder (vpon good Occasion Offred) may declare.

This Grand Nauy, of peaceable king Edgar, of so many ✲ Thousand Ships: And they furnished with a * Hundred Thousand Men, (at the least): with all the Finall Intents of those Sea-forces, (so Inuincible,) * Continually maintayned: the Order of Execution of their Seruice: The Godly & Imperiall Succes, therof: are, (in a maner,) Kingly lessons, and

H.iij.   Pro-

~~ſone~~ , Propheticall Incouragements , to vs left : (Euen now) to be as
· Prouident for Publik Security, as he was : To be as ᴸ Skilfull of our
Sea-Right, and Royall Limits : And wiſely to finde our ſelues, as Hable
to Recouer and ᴵ· Enioy the ſame , as he was : who, could not choſe , but
with the Paſſing and yeèrly Sayling about this Brytiſh Albion , with all
the LeſſerIles , next adiacent , round about it : He could not choſe (I ſay)

But by ſuch Full and * Peaceable Poſſeſſion finde him ſelf, (according to right,
and his harts deſire) the True and Souerayn Monarch , of all the Brytiſh
Ocean , enuironing any way , his Impire of Albion , and
Ireland , with the leſſer Ilands , next adiacent . With Memoriall wherof , (as with one very precious Iuell Imperiall,) he adorned the Title and Crown of his Regality: As
(with the Teſtimony annexed of the States and Nobles
of his Impire) to Commit to perpetuall Memory ,
The Stile of his chief worldly Dignity , in
this very Tenor of woords (before ,
alſo, Remembred :)

*EGO ÆDGARVS, ANGLORVM
BASILEVS, omniumq́ Regum Inſularum,
OCEANIQVE BRITANNIAM
ᴸ CIRCVMIACENTIS , Cunctarúmque
Nationum quæ infra eam includuntur,
IMPERATOR ET DOMINVS.*

What nede we , now, any better Preſident : than of a King, ſo * Iuſt,
as Edgar was , to learn, how Iuſtly, our Plat , for the Pety-Nauy-
Royall is Preſcribed, and layd owt? And, of a King, ſo *Peaceable,
as Edgar was, (And Therefore, Surnamed *PACIFICVS*,) To learn
thoſe Princely Policies, which not onely ſtand with the Due Termes of
Forreyn Peace, and Amity preſent , Royally preſerued: But, alſo, cary
with them , (Triumphantly) The Deadly Darte , and Hedding
Axe, ineuitable to all forreyn Offenders , and Homiſh Rebells?
  SOMWHAT MORE, he ſayd herein : (which I here purpoſly o-
mit:) But very much, is to be ſayd, in the Premiſſes: (As by my ſayd
Inſtructor, I perceiued not long ſynce:) which, to you, or other, in conuenient Tyme and Place, (and after his manner) he him ſelf, can beſt

1 .   expres: ᴵ· ASWELL of the Fowr conuenientPlaces, for the
ÆRARIVM PVBLICVM, or Pety-Nauy-Exchecquers, to be
                                               in :

in : (as, LONDON, YORK, WEST-CHESTER, and BRISTOW:) Both in refpect of Safe Cuftody, of the Publik-Threafor : And alfo in refpect of the Conueni-ent Diftances, from our Twenty Portes : And from the Fowr Chief Quarters, and the Hart alfo, of this ALBION : So that, Both to the fayd Exchecquers, and from them, all Payments, and Caryages, requifite, may be conueniently made:

2. As alfo, of his Plat, and *IDEA De Officijs*, Or, *De Mu-neribus Militum Naualium, & Nautarum*, of the PETY-NA-VY-ROYALL : In tyme of Peace, In tyme of Dowtfull Inclination Forrein, and in the Tyme of Open War : And that, eyther Ordinary, or Extraordinary, for the Day, for the Weke, for the Monthe, for the Quarter, and for the Yere.

3. Likewife, for the Certificat, of the Affaires, and State, of the PETY-NAVY-ROYALL, to be fent wekely, or Oftener, to our Gracious Soueraign, and her moft Vigilant Priuy Cownfailors, from the Pety-Nauy his Grand-Gouer-nor, in Tymes Sufpicious, or Dowbtfull : And but euery Fortnight, Once, in Tymes of Affured Tranquillity : And that, by fome of our Smaller Barkes : And to One of the Affigned Twenty Portes, being next to him, at that Inftant. And there, the fayd Meffager, with the Smaller Bark, to At-tend and Receiue from the Queenes Maieftie, and her Ho-norable Priuy Cownfaile, their will and pleafure : Anfwe-rable to the forfayd Certificat : And fuch farder Direction, as to them femeth for that Tyme, to be moft Expedient.

4. Fardermore, of the Prerogatiue-Prouifo Royall, very Suf-ficienly to be made, That the Grand-Gouernor, and All and euery of the Sea-Soldiers and Mariners, of the Pety-Nauy-Royall, with their Ships, fhall come in, and be in their Affigned Ports : Within any one Fortnight Space, after the Day of their Receiuing the Expres Charge, and Suf-ficient Warrant, from our Soueraign, to that Intent : Vn-les, Contrary, or Raging Storme, and Tempeft, Caufe, and Force, longer Delay. Wherein, the FAITHFVLL COM-MONS, do nothing Dowt of the Prouident-Circumfpec-tion of the Higher Powers, to Forfee, that Such Dutifull Repayre and Attendance of the Grand-Gouernor, with all his Charge, (as is here fpecifyed,) fhall be Nothing Dam-

mageable

mageable , or Preiudiciall , to the Profperous Continuance
of the Pety-Nauy-Royall , thofe his waighty Seruyces , which
partly before are fpoken of , and other , which (Yet) are
to be fpoken of. For , *Refpub. Omnis , Sua quædam habet AR-*
CANA.

5. 5. There remayne alfo , to be Declared , the Reafons , why
my Inftructor doth Wifh , and Aduife , Parte of the Publik -
Threafory , to be beftowed vpon fome Two , or Three Honeft Men , who fhould be Skilfull in Far-Forreyn-Langua -
ges : As , in the Sclauonian , or Mofchouite , the Arabik
Vulgar , the Turkifh , the Tartarien , the Chiny Language ,
the Canadien , and the Iflandifh , &c . For that , (within
☞ thefe few yeares next following,) with Men of all thefe
Cuntries , and farder , Great Affayres are by fome of our Cun-
try-Men to be handled : Yf God contynue his Gracious
Direction , and Ayde thereto , as he hath very Cumfortably
begonne .

6. 6. And fome alfo , of the fayd Pety-Nauy-Threafor , he did
Affigne , for a good Stypend geuing to an Excellent Enginer ,
afwell for Matters of Fortification , as alfo , for Inuenting
of Weapons , or Engyns , Offenfiue , or Defenfiue , by Land ,
or Sea : And likewife , for Engyns of Seruice , for Profit-
Publik , otherwife : By Land , and Sea : Either aboue Grownd
and Water , or vnder Grownd and Water , &c .

7. 7. Moreouer , fome Parte to be beftowed on Fowr Chriftian Philofophers , Skilfull , or to become Skilfull , and alfo
Excellent : both in Speculation , and alfo Practife , of the beft
Manner of the Ancient and Secret Philofophie : which is
not Vulgar : but , Vndowtedly , which may be moft Com-
☞ fortable , and Profitable , to Some , of Courteous KALID ,
his Difpofition , &c . By which Titles of Matter , left Vnfpe-
cifyed hitherto , It may Euidently appere , that my Inftructor
hath (as it were ,) but opened the Doore of his Philofo -
phicall and Politicall Brytifh Furniture : to be Fauorably
vewed of them , whofe Infight , is Sharp , and Pro -
found : Whofe Zeale , and Care alfo , for the State-
Publik of this Monarchy , to become moft
Chriftianlike Happy , (in all Refpects ,)
is Ardent , and not Luke-warme .

Seeing then

Seeing then, {

NO KINGDOM , in thefe Dayes , hath more nede of a PETY-NAVY-ROY-ALL, and to be Continually at Sea maintayned , for the Refpects aboue rehearfed :

No Kingdome , hath apter TYMBER for Shipping : And thereof (YET) ftore enough :

No Kingdome , hath Skilfuller , and more SHIP-WRIGHTS :

No Kingdome , hath Subiects better HA-BLE, and which more willingly will be Contributary for the fufficient Setting forth , and mayntenance of fuch a PETY-NAVY-ROYALL , continually , at Sea (and that , for the former Refpects :)

No Kingdome , hath better ftore of APT and willing MEN : as well couragious Ientlemen , as other : very manfully difpofed , to furnifh the forefayd Nauy with , for all kynde of purpofes :

No Kingdome , hath better , or more Hauens, and HARBOROVGHS, (and thofe , round about it) to Succour a Nauy in , from Dangers , or Diftres of Sea :

No King, nor Kingdome , hath , by Nature and Humayn Induftry (to be v-fed) any , more LAWFVLL, and more Peaceable Means (made euident)wherby, to become , In wealth, far pafsing all other : In Strength , and Force, INVINCIBLE : and in Honorable eftimation, Triumphantly Famous , ouer all , and aboue all other :

} Than this hath :

And , (To be brief) Seeing No Kingdome,

is more Diſcrete, and willing to Vſe the * Opportunity, of any exceding great and Publik Benefit procuring to the ſame, than this Brytiſh Monarchy, is, or May be: Our hope, then is, That, vpon
the Vniforme, Brotherly, Willing, and Frank Conſent, of all States, of
Men and People, of this Incomparable Realme of England: to this Godly, Politik, and moſt Commendable Means: to preſerue Amity and
Peace, with all Forreyn Princes: And to Garde this State-Publik in Security, from taking Iniury of any, or by any, (Fraudulently, or Forci-
bly,) And to kepe our own hands and harts, from Dooing, or Intending Iniury, to any Forreyner, on Sea or Land: Our Hope is, (ſayd
he,) That vpon this Godly Intente, Diſcrete Couenant, and Publik
Contributary Oblation: the Omnipotent + Author of Heauenly Peace,
will ſo bend down his Mercifull and gratious Eyes, vpon vs: and ſo ma-
nifeſtly ſtretch forth his Almighty hand to Bles, Furder, and Proſper
the foreſayd Oblation, with all the Purpoſes and Commodities therof expeded, and likely to enſue : that, all we may, with the
Kingly Prophet *Dauid*, (both old and yong, Rich and Poore,)
moſt ioyfully, and Triumphantly, (*IN PERFECT
SECVRITIE,*) Syng,

*Lauda HIERVSALEM Dominum,
    Lauda Deum tuum SION.
Quoniam confortauit Seras Portarum tuarum :
    Benedixit filijs tuis in te.
Qui poſuit fines tuos PACEM,
    Et adipe Frumenti ſatiat te. &c.
Non fecit Taliter omni Nationi.*

O Hieruſalem, prayſe the Lord : Prayſe thy God,
O Syon . For, he hath Strengthened the Barres of
thy Gates, And hath bleſſed thy Children within
thee ; He hath made all thy Borders *PEACE* :
And with the good Nutriment of wheat, doth
ſatiſfy thee. &c. He hath not done thus, to
euery Nation, els : Prayſe we all,
the Lord therefore.
Amen.

Omewhat, I haue now ſayd, (quoth my Inſtructor) in this PETY NAVY MATTER: to diſcharge me of my Duty, to the COMMON-WELTH, herein : And very ſory I am , that I know not, as much, as this moſt waighty Caſe requireth , to be * Speedily known: And that I am not able, aptly and Duly to Order and expres ſo much, as I already know . And moſt of all, I Dowt, that ſome men will ſtick to performe , or ſhrinke to prefer, or be Careles to amend this Simple Plat : of me ; ſpeedily, zealouſly, and vnartificially * deliuered to the pen, and very Briefly, expreſſed.

*Speede.

Moreouer, (ſayd he) if it ſhould not be taken in worſe parte, of OVR SOVERAIGN, than , of the Emperour of Conſtantinople, *Emanuel*, the ſyncere Intent, and faythfull Aduiſe, of *Georgius Gemiſtus Pletho*, was, I could (proportionally, for the occaſion of the Tyme, and place,) frame and ſhape ſ. very much of *Gemiſtus* thoſe his two Greek Orations, (the firſt, to the Emperor, and the Second to his Sonne, Prince *Theodore* :) for our BRYTISH ILES, and in better and more allowable manner, at this Day, for our People, than that his Plat (for Reformation of the State, at thoſe Dayes,) could be found, for *Peloponneſus*, auaylable . But, Seeing thoſe Orations, are now publiſhed : both in Greek and Latin, I need not Dowbt, but they, to whom, the chief Care of ſuch cauſes is committed, haue Diligently ſelected the Hony of thoſe Flowres, already , for the Common-Wealths great Benefit. But, *Gemiſtus* ſayd very well, THEN:

* *Anno Domini 1 5 7 8. Auguſti primis ſex diebus: And therefore, this Treatiſe in other places, is called Hexameron*

ſ. Though in ſundry points, my Inſtructor did miſlike Gemiſtus opinion : ſometymes not the ſoundeſt for the Peloponneſians commoditie: & ſomtimes greatly repugnant to the order moſt nedeful for this Brytiſh Policy: Yet, much therof, might be a good Aduiſe for the framing of an Analogical Ciuile conſideration, in reſpect of the Intent, by Gemiſtus regarded.

GEORGII GEMISTI PLE-
thonis de Rebus Peloponneſi,
ORATIO. I.

Ellum quidem cum *Jtalis* , *Peloponneſum* tenentibus à præſtantiſſimis filijs geſtum, magna cum Laude, et Emolumento confectum eſt, (*Jmperator Auguſte:*) Cùm & plurima maximéq; opportuna illorum Dominia, noſtram in poteſtatem, longo poſt tempore redierint : & ipſi, cùm reliqua nobis omnia ceſſerint , tùm in vniuerſum ſe nobis obtemperaturos receperint. Quibus ex rebus, vobis quidem hoc pacto Imperium & confirmantibus & augentibus, decus et gloria: nobis autem, *SECVRITAS* naſcitur, & Vtilitas: Maiorúmq; in poſterum conſequendorum, (Si Deus permiſerit) Occaſio. Mihi verò, *nunc ea tibi exponere in mentem venit, quæ multis de Cauſis arbitror , ſi obſeruentur, multum his rebus eſſe profutura: ſiue negligantur, magnam Salutis partem detractura. Ac primùm de ipſa Regione, quanti ſit vobis facienda, pauca quædam dicam: non tàm quòd veſtrum erga ipſam ſtudium non videam , quàm vt ipſa recto ordine procedat Oratio. Etenim, Nos quibus Imperatis, Græci genere ſumus: vt par-

* *Circa Annum Domini, 1400.*

tim, è Sermone, partim ex auita Disciplina constare potest . Græcis
verò vix vlla magis familiaris reperiri possit Regio quàm PELO-
PONNESVS, & quæcunq; iuxta hanc ad Europam spectant,
quæq adiacent Insulæ. Hanc enim Terram, quantùm humana potest
memoria recolere, ijdem semper à nullis antè possessam incoluerunt Græci: Nec Aduenæ eam occuparunt, eiectis aliis, ipsiq nonnunquam ab
alijs eiecti : sed contrà, semper hanc Regionem tenuerunt Græci, nec
deseruerunt vnquam . Iam, inter omnes huius Regionis partes, Pelo-
ponnesum, præcipuas ac nobilissimas Græcorum gentes protulisse tra-
ditur: ex eáq Græcos profectos, maximas ac præclarissimas quásq; res
gessisse . Quid quòd magnæ quoq; istius ad Bosporum sitæ.* Vrbis,
(quæ vestra nunc est Regia,) terram hanc, qui rectè rem consideret,
quasi Matrem, non iniuria dixerit . Nam & qui antè, Byzantium
incoluerunt, Græci fuerunt ac Dores: (Dores autem, Peloponnesios
esse, Nemini dubium est:) Et qui posterioribus Sæculis illustrem illam
ex Italica Roma deduxerant Coloniam, tamq præclaro Byzantium
auxerunt Additamento, non sunt à Peloponnesys alieni. Siquidem, vt
Æneadæ & Sabini pari Iure permisti, Romanam Vrbem fœlicissi-
mam incoluerunt, Jta Sabini censentur Peloponnesÿ de Lacedæmonÿs
profecti . Quocirca, nec his de causis parui facienda tàm vobis, quàm
nobis, est hæc Regio: Quandoquidem & maximè propria, curanda sunt maximè : Et hæc omnium est maximè Propria . Et, si de
ipsius virtute, qua nulli Terræ cedit, dicendum est, vt ea quæ de Anni temporum temperie, deq Terra nascentium, & omnium ad vitam
pertinentium prouentu dici possint, nunc omittam : AD SECV-
☞ RITATEM sanè, nullam non Regionem hæc superat: cum & In-
,, sula pariter tanta sit, & Continens . Nec difficulter possint eius In-
,, colæ, si rectè suppetentibus vtantur adiumentis, cum apparatu mini-
,, mo, si quis inuadat, repellere: Tùm ad alios, vbi videatur ipsi, accedere : itáq Regionis terminos non leuiter augere. Prætereà, nunc
Montium munimenta, qui per totam porriguntur terram, & vbiq
(Arcium instar) eminent, sic vt hostes, etiamsi Campestri solo fortè
potiantur, tota tamen excidant Regione . Quo fit, vt non tàm fami-
liaritatis, quàm virtutis ipsius causa curanda videatur hæc Regio:
,, Quandoquidem possessiones potiores, potius etiam studium solent requi-
rere . Jam cùm omnibus, qui inter Græcos censentur, hæc impendit Cura, tùm Regibus maximè, quibus vniuersi Tutela, præ cæ-
teris, est commissa . Neminem porrò superiorum Regum, pro-
pius quàm Te, hæc Res attingit . Nam & cùm Jtali ditionem
hanc tenerent, in eáq longo tempore Regnassent, soli eam vestræ Familiæ Principes recuperarunt . Et ipse Tu, præter alia multa magnáq
Beneficia, præclarum illud atq; ingens Opus nuper erexisti, ducto per
Isthmum * Muro: maxima & præstantissima Perpetuæ Salutis oc-
casione

*Constanti-
nopolis.

Murus per
Isthmum du-
ctus.

cafione . Quocircà vos decet , cum priorum Beneficiorum collocatione , hęc etiam confequentia coniungere : quò fimul & ipfi rerum pręclararùm augmento ftudere videamini, & ipfa à vobis ante collata beneficia, perpetuitate Confequentium , falua permaneant . Neque parùm , tùm SECVRITATIS *, tùm Emolumenti , magnę quoq; ifti vrbi (vt arbitror)hęc Regio rectè conftituta adferet : id quod , hoc quidem loco pluribus explicare fupervacaneum nobis videtur . Ac ftudium quidem fummum hanc mereri Regionem , fatis à me , quantùm res poftulat , demonftratum exiftimo : Quam autem cupiam diligentiam , cum prioribus veftris coniungi Beneficijs , quǽq; harum rerum corrigendæ potiffimùm videantur , quoq́; illæ pacto compofitæ , plurimùm fint fructus allaturę , nunc aperiam : fi ea priùs , quæ in his minus rectè habent , explicuero . Primum itaq. &c.*

And agayn:

Quocirca , priufquam tale quid eueniat, Decet nos , dum in Tu-   Pag. 213.
to Sumus , & quę minus rectè videntur fe habere , corrigere : & , quantùm Liceat , Neceffaria præparare : ne , Si quis forte cafus accidat , eum difficulter feramus . Nam , in ipfo quidem difcrimine ,non fatis commodè correctionem , fi quę requirunt , recipiunt . &c.

SECVRITATEM *deniq̧ vniverfis pręftant Milites , &*   Pag. 214.
Præfecti, *quiq̧ alij alias Reipub. partes curant: fingulaq̧ tùm parua, tùm magna conferuant: & præcipuus* REX ,*omnibus* Imperans, omniáq̧; gubernans , & conferuans &c.

Quòd fi quid fanè aliud , melius pariter et facilius , ab alio fubijciatur ,   Pag. 218.
illud fequendum erit . Contemnenda certè res ifta nòn eft: nec in hoc ftatu prauo , fimul & periculofo , reliquenda . Atqui nec melius nec vtilius quenquam , quid aliud , eo', quod à me prolatum eft , reperturum aio: Neq̧ difficulter ad effectum id perduci poffe : aut potiùs , difficulter , hoc in ftatu , res iftas diutiùs , abfq̧ magno periculo & incommodo , durare poffe . Tuum porrò duntaxat , Imperator , pręcipuum oportet accedere calculum . Neq; difficulter facies , vt , cùm ipfe Rebus prępfis omnibus , quæ optima fimul ac Iuftifsima videantur , ac tùm publicè, tùm priuatim omnibus vtilifsima , conftituas . &c.

Atque Ego quidem quę fore vtilia cenfeo , quibufq̧; de Caufis, dixi! Et , vt , eadem etiam præftantifsimis filijs tuis , hac Orationis forma expofui : ita , Tuum præcipuè requirunt Calculum : quem, tanquam ab aliquo fortita Numine , fimul & honefta videantur , & ad exitum perducantur : Faxit autem Deus , vt eum qui & profit , & vndecunq̧; rectè fe habeat , Calculum feras.

And Bycaufe , in *Gemiſtus* , his Second Oration , to Prince *Theodore* , (this Emperour his Sonne) there are many thinges , (In my Inftructor his Opinion) woorth the knowledge and Confideration : and not vtterly vnapt for this place : And for that, it fhould be a Difgrace, fo to mangle the whole matter, and a hynderance to the vnderftanding therof : to break of, the particular Notes , fo often, from the other Circumftances of woords, and Sentences annexed in the courfe of the fame Oration , as thinges fall owt, Notable : And bycaufe, this way, the very whole * Text of the fayd Oration, may eafier be had, than from beyond the Seas, (as they are,) in Greeke and Latin prynted : I thought it fome Reafonable Caufe. why, I fhould, here, fet down the fame Oration, whole : that, whofoeuer fhould mete with the Memorials of thefe Difcourfes, nede not want the fame, if it be to his Liking.

(⁂)

ΤΟΥ ΑΥΤΟΥ ΠΛΗΘΩΝΟΣ

ΣΥΜΒΟΥΛΕΥΤΙΚΟΣ ΠΡΟΣ ΤΟΝ ΔΕΣΠΟΤΗΝ ΘΕΟΔΩ-ΡΟΝ, ΠΕΡΙ ΤΗΣ ΠΕΛΟΠΟΝΝΗΣΟΥ.

GEORGII GEMISTI PLE-thonis ad Principem Theodorum de Rebus Peloponnes: Oratio Posterior: GVLIELMO CANTERO, Interprete.

Vm in Naui Gubernator, omnia pro suo solet arbitrio dirigere, quæ ad Vectorum Salutem pertinet: Tùm in Exercitu, Dux, quæ ad Militum victoriam. (Alioqui nec Vectoribus, nec Militibus, vel tantillo tempore res rectè procederent, nisi ab Vno vtræq; viro regerentur: & apertissimè, maximis in periculis, Monarchiam, simul tutissimam & vtilissimam deprehendimus:) Veruntamen, et in Naui Licere videmus * Vectorum alicui, qui consilio suo communem videatur Salutem iuuare posse: et in excercitu, Militi similiter: illi quidem apud Gubernatorem, huic autem ante Ducem, quæ in mentem venerint exponere. Illis porrò cùm audierint, vel arripere Licet consilium, vel benignè et sine acerbitate reijcere. Siquidem non iniquè ferendum est, Siquis in Periculo communi, Salutis publicæ curam ad se quoq; nonnihil arbitretur pertinere. Enimuerò hac quoque in Gente nostra, atque Vrbe, tibi quidem, vir Clarissime, totius est rei cura commissa: peráq; multorum maiorum, Regum, Patris´q, etiam Regis, manus, hæc ad te deuenit nostræ Regionis hæreditas: in qua tibi omnia, prout tibi ac nobis videantur profutura, Licet omniú pleno consensu disponere. Cum autem tuæ quidem sic se res habeant, nostræ autem in magno versentur discrimine: (Siquidem, vndique no-

I.iij.   bis,

---

*

The maner hovv a Subiect may dutifully say his mynde, in Matters, besides, or aboue his Charge and gouernment.

Cicero his wordes to the like intent may aptly herewith be conferred: Te ipsum monet Pansa (quanquam non eges consilio, quo Vales plurimú: tamé etiã summi Gubernatores in magnis tempestatibus, à Vectoribus admoneri solent) huic tuum tantum apparatum, iamq; præclarum ne ad nihilum recidere patiare. Tempus habet tale, quale vnmo habuit Vnquam. Hac grauitate Senatus; hoc studio Equestris Ordinis, hoc ardore Pop. Ro. potes in perpetuum metu & periculo Rempub. liberare. Cicero: Philippica. 7.

* Vide supra
Pag. 53.
Linea. 30.

bis, *Terra Mariq́ tenduntur* Insidiæ : adeóque *Domi* etiam *à Barba-*
ris simul & *Gentilibus* , maximè autem à vicinis istis *Barbaris* , qui
etiam reliqui *Dominy* maximam ac potissimam partem nobis ademerunt : & *Parapamisadæ* origine cum sint , & obiter ab *Alexandro*
Philippi F. deuicti , cum is ad *Indos* tenderet , à nobis nunc , tanquam
Græcis , longo quidem pòst tempore , multiplices autem horum pœnas
expetunt : Cumq́ longè præstent viribus , extrema nobis queq́ semper minantur.) Cùm igitur hæc ita se habeant , non absurdè mihi fac-
turus videor , Si , cùm de *Salute communi* paulo melius fortasse ,
quàm cæteri , sentire videar : ad te , *Principem nostrum* , accedam ,
queq́ tibi simul et nobis omnibus existimem *Salutaria* fore , subijci-
☞ am. *Illud autem primùm à te petam , si forte non Totus Sermo vo-*
„ *luptate sit conditus , verùm aliquid etiam subsultet asperius , vt me*
„ *præstantiora & vtiliora patiaris iucundis præferre . Nam ne Me-*
„ *dicos quidem video , cùm Salus ægrotantium agitur , vel acerbissimis*
„ *cibis , potibus , & Pharmacis alijs abstinere : Contráque , Coquos ple-*
„ *runq́ obsoniorum Voluptate , corpus etiam corrumpere . Adeò non*
„ *semper quæ iucunda , sunt vtilia : verùm iuuant etiam acerbissima.*

Atq́ hoc primum est existimandum , nec priuatis hominibus , nec *Re-*
buspub. vel in maximis difficultatibus , de meliori fortuna esse desperandum . Siquidem permulti sunt in integrum restituti . Nam &
Troiani, qui cum *ÆEnea* , capta à *Græcis* patria , in *Italiam* sunt ex
Phrygia delati , ita prosperam deinde sunt experti fortunâ , *Vt* , cùm
Romam paulò post vnà cum *Sabinis* , de *Lacedæmonijs* profectis ,
pari iure permistis , incoluissent , ab hoc principio maximum pariter
& præclarissimum obtinuerint *Imperium* . Et *Persæ* , post *Alexandri*
Græcorumq́ dominium , Cùm à *Romanis* esset euersa *Macedonum*
potentia , non leuiter & ipsi *Parthorum* ope suas recuperarunt *Vires* :
sed vt etiam contra *Romanos* , qui tum erant potentissimi , bellum
gesserint : & vt nonnunquam superati fuerint , ita postremò splendi-
dam reportarint victoriam : ex eáque multis annis *Tributum* quoque
Romanis imperarint . Quocirca nec nos decet nosmetipsos abijcere ,
vel de *Salute* desperare : Sed cùm & ipsi post has ærumnas meliora
speremus , illud etiam omni diligentia considerare , quibus modis ad
SECVRITATEM aliquam res nostræ reducantur , & meliorem pro facultate nostra statum nobis comparemus . Vt autem meliorem sibi statum vel *Ciuitas* vel *Gens* aliqua firmiter , (quantùm quidem res humanæ ferunt ,) comparet , non alia res efficit , quam *REI.*
PVBL: EMENDATIO . Nulla siquidem alia *Ciuitatibus*
est vel *fælicitatis* vel *infælicitatis* causa , quàm *Resp.* rectè vel secus
constituta . Quòd si qua Casu rectè se *Ciuitas* habeat , id firmum non
est , ac leui de causa potest immutari . Plerunque autê , vel bona † *Rep.*
conseruantur & crescunt *Ciuitates* : vel contrà , corrupta , & ipsæ col-
labun-

„ + δ l ἀ περὶ ω
πολιτείας.

labuntur ac pereunt . *Nam & communiter Græci non antè la-*
tiſſimè patentem obtinuerunt gloriam, quàm Hercules Amphitryonis ‟
F. Iniuſtitia Sublata , bonam Reipublicæ conſtitutionem , virtutiſque ‟
ſtudium ipſis conciliauit . (*Siquidem ante Herculem quidem non val-* ‟
dè fuit celebre Græcorum genus, cui Danai , & Cadmi , ex Barba-
ria aduenę , imperarent : poſt Herculem autem, multas Gręci mag-
náſq; tùm à Græcis, tùm à Barbaris retulerunt victorias :) *& Lace-*
dæmonij non antè vel Græcorum facti ſunt Principes , quàm à Ly-
curgo pręclaram illam Reip: conſtitutionem acciperent : vel Principa-
tu pulſi exciderunt , quàm eandem negligerent , ac tum ſibi Maris im-
perium vindicarent , qui terram eatenus tenuerant : tùm equitatu mi-
nimùm valerent : quem vt alebant ditiſſimi quiq; , ita belli tempore ,
alijs , cum armis qualibuſcunq; tradebant : tùm ſociis non clementer am-
plius imperaret. Quocirca ſunt à Thebanis deuicti, ductu Epaminondæ,
qui Doctrinam Pythagoricam non ſegniter perceperat. Philippus quoq;*
ab hoc Epaminonda , cum Thebis Obſes degeret , inſtitutus, Græcorum
Princeps euaſit : nec non eius F. Alexander, cùm Philippi patris , tùm
Ariſtotelis inſuper inſtitutione, & Græcorum Imperium , & Aſiæ Reg-
num ſuperatis Perſis ſibi comparauit . Quinetiam Romani ad maxi-*
mum Principatum, Reip. bonitate peruenerunt : nec prius res illorum
labi cœperunt , quàm Remp. immutaſſent. Saraceni deniq; iſti olim qui-
dem parua quædam erant Arabum pars , & Romanis ferè parebant :
Poſtquam verò mutata Rep. leges quaſdam ferri ſibi paſſi ſunt , quæ
vt non ad aliud quicquam , ſaltem ad Ciuitatum augmentum & belli-
cas victorias viderentur conducere : Primùm Gentilium Arabum nacti
ſunt Imperium , deinde Romanorum dominio maximam & potiſſimam
ademerunt partem : tum Africam ſibi adiecerunt : poſtremò Perſas in
ſuam redegerunt poteſtatem. Sed & aliæ Gentes aliquot , horum vten-
tes moribus & ritibus , fœlicitate frui videntnr. Atque adeò iſti , qui
nobis plurimùm præſtiterunt , Barbari his vtentes legibus maxima po-
tentia polluerunt. Eodem ferè pacto , ſi quis reliqua conſideret, & Gen-
tes & vrbes reperiet ex bonis vel malis Rebuſpublicis, rectè ſe vel ſe-
cus habuiſſe. Quare, ſi hoc videbitur conſiderandum, quibus modis tùm
ad Salutem perueniamus , tùm potiorem ſtatum nobis comparemus :
Emendanda duntaxat eſt Reſpublica, prauis inſtitutis in rectiora com-
mutatis.

  Iam , cùm ſint multa quæ Rempub . conſtituant , eamq́; ſingu-
la vel meliorem vel peiorem efficiant, nimirum quæ plurimis & potiſ-
ſimis conſtabit melioribus , proba futura eſt Reſpub. quæ ijſdem pe-
ioribus , improba. Ac primùm, quia Rerump. tria ſunt genera, Mo-
narchicum, Oligarchicum , & Democraticum : Pluresq́; item ſingulo-
rum ſpecies, quibus vel corrigitur vel corrumpitur Reſp. Prudentiſſi-
mi ſanè quiq́; Monarchiam, Conſultoribus optimis et legibus probis, ijſq́;

Doctrina Py-
thagorica Re-
buſpub. vtiliſſi-
ma.

MONARCHIA

I. iiij.   ratis

ratis ῦtentem, cunɛ̃is prætulerunt.

Consultores.

Ac de Consultoribus quidem, primùm, Eruditorum hominum laudatur moderata Copia. Nam & ῦulgus, quoniam difficulter inter se intelligunt, multofᶙ habet indoɛ̃os, temerarios plerunᶙ fert calculos: Et qui pauciβimo conſtant numero, cùm Priuatim feɛ̃entur Lucrum, praua dant ferè Conſilia. At qui ſimul & moderato numero fuerint, & non indoɛ̃i, cùm ῦt alius aliud conſideret, atque in medium proferat, ita Communi ῦtilitate communiter ducantur, optimi erunt ac certiβimi Conſultores. Deindè hoc requiritur, ῦt mediocri ſint fortuna, nec ῦel ditiβimi ῦel pauperrimi: ſiquidem illi, præ diuitiarum ſtudio, nihil ferè ſuadent aliud, quàm ῦnde Lucrum ipſis aliquod proueniat: hi, præ inopia, nihil ſpeɛ̃ant aliud, quàm ῦt Neceſsitati ſubueniant ſuæ. At qui ſe mediocriter habent, Communem potiβimùm Salutem curant. Ac de Conſultoribus quidem, hacɛ̃enus.

Leges.

Leges verò, probæ ſunt, ῦt ῦno verbo dicam, quæ ſua ſingulis, tùm in Vrbe, tùm in Gente quauis, officia definientes, alienis negotÿs ῦetent ſe immiſcere.

Ruſtici.

Atᶐ in omni ferè Ciuitate, Primum & maxime Neceſsarium eſt, et Numeroſiβimum, Ruſticorum genus: Agricolarum videlicet, Paſtorum, quiᶙ alÿ Terræ fruɛ̃us proprÿs manibus colligunt. Alterum eſt Opificum genus, Mercatorum. Inſtitorum, & ſimilium: quod primis illis ac reliquæ Ciuitati inſeruit: dum Opifices quidem Supelleɛ̃ilem humanæ vitæ neceſsariam, in medium producunt: Mercatores autem, quæ ſingulis Regionibus ῦel deſint ῦel ſuperſint, de ῦna in aliam transferendo Exæquant: & quoniam alÿ ſuis coguntur rebus vacare, ipſi hanc Prouinciam ſuſcipiunt: Jnſtitores deniᶐ, de Ruſticis quidem, ῦel Mercatoribus emunt ῦniuerſa: requirentibus autem ſingulis, quandöcunᶐ & quocunᶐ velint numero, diuendunt. Nonnulli etiam corporis ῦires elocantes, nunc his nunc illis miniſterium exhibendo viɛ̃itant.

Opifices.

Mercatores.

Inſtitores.

Laborers.

Principes.

REX.

Poſtremum eſt Principum genus, qui ῦel Vrbem, ῦel Gentem totam conſeruant, atᶐ cuſtodiunt. Quorum, ῦt ſupremus eſt Rex, ita poſt illum, alÿ alias Vrbis ῦel Gentis ſortiti partes, ritè conſeruant. Cùm enim hoc omnibus perſuaderi nequeat, æquitatem abſᶙ iniuria ſeɛ̃andam eſse, nec tendendas cuiuſquam bonis inſidias: Nonnulli autem, ῦel primi ῦel ſecundi generis, omiβis operibus ſuis, aliorum inhient laboribus: Contra hos, inſtituti ſunt, ex amicis quidem, Iudices, & reliqui Præfeɛ̃i: ex inimicis verò, Milites, & horum Duces. Quibus, cùm, tanquam publicæ intentis cuſtodiæ, aliundè ſuppeditanda eſsent neceſsaria, Tributa Ruſticis, in Dimenſum Publicorum Cuſtodum, imperata ſunt: Merces pariter et Præmium Cuſtodiæ futura. Atque hæc Tributorum eſt origo.

Iudices.

Milites.

Tributorum Origo.

Cùm porrò, tria hæc prima ſunt hominum in ῦrbe genera, propria quædam ſingulorum eſse debent officia: quæ quidem proba Lex obire
                                                                        quemᶙ

quemq; iubet, nec inter se confundere. Principes igitur nullum subeant Ministerium, quandoquidem Imperio maximè contrarium est ministrare. Sunt autem inter Ministeria, cùm alia quæ recensuimus, tum Institoria & Mercatura. At Principem iubet Lex, nec Mercaturam nec Institoriam facere, nec aliud quicquam non liberale tractare. Similiter à Vulgo secernantur Milites, ac Seruatores à seruandis: & illi quidem ab omni Collatione liberi Militent, ac Populum tueantur: Hi verò suas res agentes idonea, simul nec grauia Principum & Militum delectorum Dimenso, Tributa pendant. Maior vero pars Exercitus & potior, Ciuium sit ac domesticorum, non Peregrinorum: siquidem raro fidi sunt Peregrini, multisq; mutationibus: interdum pro Seruatoribus atq; Custodibus hostes existunt. Domestici verò si rectè curentur, magis firmi sunt atq; fidi. De Rusticis autem pleriq; militiæ assueti, per coniugationes diuidantur, eorumq; alterutro communibus ferè laborante sumptibus, vicissim alter laboret, alter militet: sic vt pariter et familiæ suæ curam & Salutis Communis ijdem, quantum fieri possit, gerant. Separentur autem in exercitu Pedites ab Equitibus: Peditibus quidem in Turmas sub Ducibus, Equitibus autem in Alas sub Magistris relatis, quò confestim possint, vbicunq; fuerit opus, ordine adesse. Neque simul vtreq; Copiæ, Terrestres ac Nauales, cogantur: verùm alteræ semper, eæq; * Si id Vrbis & Gentis atq; etiam Regionis patiatur Natura, potiùs terrestres: ne cum vtrisq; simus inferiores, neutros vincamus. Ac præstat longe * Terrestribus Copijs in militum ac Ducum virtute, quam Nautarum ac aliorum hominum † vilium arte fiduciam ponere: ac terra potitos, indidem necessaria nancisci, quàm peregrè petere: relictisq; Mari proximis locis, nisi cogat extrema necessitas, soli cum vicinis bello vacare: quàm pluribus, tùm cum vicinis, tùm cum exteris. Iam cùm Tributorum tria sint minimùm genera, Primum Seruitus, deinde certa siue pecuniæ, siue aliarum rerum summa, tùm quædam rerum nascentium pars: Grauissimum quidem Tributi genus est Seruitus, quippe quod non opes arripiat, sed corpora: nec paruam ipsis præbet exactoribus molestiam, quorum præsentiam quotannis requirit: certa verò summa, præter seruitutem, magnam etiam habet inæqualitatem, dum & necessariò penditur, et sæpè non pro opibus: quando nec facilè sit opibus cuiusq; Tributum exæquare, nec singulorum opes eandem semper obtineant magnitudinem. (Eadem quidem per partes quotannis sæpiùs à pluribus exacta, longè maiorem difficultatem parit.) Rerum autem nascentium quædam pars cùm seruitutis minus habet, tùm quouis alio Tributo, tantundem quod efficeret, multo leuior est, ipsa temporis ratione, (quandoquidem, quo tempore fructus à singulis colliguntur, de ipsis petitur fructibus:) nec non æqualitatem habet maximam, dùm quisq; pro opibus persoluit: quo fit, vt optimum sit hoc Tributum; cùm & leuissimum

* Marke this sir for, in our Ilandish State, certainly and euidently, our greater aduantage and les cost and encombrance is to kepe our Publike and vniuersall Garde in a Navy at Sea. As before is aboundantly proued. And GEMISTVS his earnest desire to prefer the Land forces, and Land Soldiers maketh him to speake not so aptly and honorably as the Case might admit of skilfull Sea-men and Mariners: who alone are not the workers of great victories at Sea without the Sea Soldiers industry and valiantnes concurrent. For his Cuntry, and at that Tyme (perhaps) it was best so, to refuse the maintenance of a Navy. And after this manner, are many things in this oration: which, at that Tyme, and in that Place, were for the Peloponnesians more [illegible] and commodious, than the like were to be deemed for this State. For, all, here, conteined, is not to be of vs allowed, or imitated: But here and there, the Idea generall, is to be answered with due application, particularly, for our Cuntry, and these our Dayes.

† φαύλων.

mum fit, vt diximus, & æquißimum: &, fi cum æquitate exigatur, Reipubl. vtilißimum.

Quæ porrò æquitas híc locum habeat, hinc licet animaduertere. Terræ fructus tria potißimùm requirunt, Operas, Sumptus operis præbendos, (vt boues, vineas, Armenta, et fimilia) & horum Cuftodiam. Quapropter ètiam Tribus iure debentur, Operis, fumptuum Dominis, ac deniq̃ Cuftodibus vniuerforum et Seruatoribus, quos Reges, Principes, aliofq̃ Præfectos diximus. Ruftici ergo, qui fuis laborant fumptibus, cùm liceat ipfis quocunq; loco, terram quouis pacto colere, duabus fruentes partibus, altera operis, altera fumptibus debita, Tertiam Reipubl. et Cuftodibus vniuerforum præftent: omni alia Collatione quacunque omniq̃ minifterio vacantes. Atq; hoc fit iuftißimum Tributum, Præmium fimul ac Dimenfum publicis miniftris futurum. Ac de Tributis quidem hactenus.

Viuendi porrò ratio, cùm reliquorum Ciuium, tùm Præfectorum maximè, non fumptuofa, fed moderata fit: fic vt peregrinas quidem veftes et nugas alias negligant: ad Bellum autem fint omnes compofiti, quiq̃ huc pertinent apparatus, diligenter procurent: quos quidem, cùm aliò fumptus transferuntur, diminui oportet ac deteri.

Terræ fructus nemini liceat, quocunque velit, nifi alteram partem pro vectigali pendat, euehere. Ad focios quidem, euehere liceat. Sin quis ferro, vel armis, vel alia re neceffaria velit mutare, nihil pendat.

Moneta nec improba nec peregrina vtamur: ne videamur etiam praua & aliena vti Republica. Siquidem non paruum in Republica momentum habet Monetæ ratio.

Sontes ne Barbarico more mulctentur, vt poft mulctam minimùm deinceps peccent. Nam qui videntur infanabiles effe, eos de medio præftat auferentes, animam corpore liberare, qua non recte nouit vti: quàm illos mutilantes, hanc tùm corpori mutilo atq̃ inutili, tùm reliquæ Ciuitati alligare.

Atq; hæ quidem probæ funt Reipubl. Leges, aliæq̃ fimiles: Caput autem horum eft omnium, de Deo recte & publicè et priuatim fentire, maximè autem hæc tria: Primùm, effe Deum quendam præftantißimam omnium Naturam: deinde, hunc & homines curare, et res omnes humanas tùm magnas, tùm paruas regere: tùm arbitrio fuo cuncta illum recte iufteq̃ femper adminiftrare, nufquam ab officio deflectentem, vel alia de caufa, vel hominum donis delinitum, quibus non indigeat. Quæ cùm ita fe habent, confequitur illud, vt in cultu facra donariaq̃ modo & pietate adhibitis offerant, velut inde bonum omne proficifci fatentes: nec vel minùs præftantes, aut duarum, aut alterius faltem duarum impietatis formarum opinionem fibi comparent: vel nimio fumptu, & priuatas domos & Rempubl. perdentes,

quafi

quaſi donariorum quicquam proficeret magnificentia : nec ampliu$ quid offerre, ſed redimere viſi, tertio ſe impietatis generi obſtringunt. Has demum ſententias publicè priuatim$\acute{q}$, confirmatas, neceſſariò virtus & honeſti omne ſtudium ſequitur.

At vitium quoduis et maxima mortalium peccata, de contrarijs naſcuntur ſententijs. Semper enim exiſtunt nonnulli prauis opinionibus imbuti: & vel nullum eſſe prorſus Deum arbitrantes, vel vt ſit, res tamen humanas negligere: vel deniq; vt ſit atque curet, corrumpi nihilominus poſſe, ſacriſ$\acute{q}$ ac donarijs delinitum, nonnunquam ab officio deflectere.

Ab his enim duabus inter ſe contrarijs de Deo ſententijs, tanquam fontibus, duo procedunt vitæ genera, plurimùm inter ſe diſſidentia: quorum alterum virtutem vel ſolum, vel ſummum ponit bonum, alterum Voluptatem.

Etenim cùm Hominis natura, partim Diuina ſit, partim humana, (quod omnibus & Græcis & Barbaris vel aliqua præditis mente viſum fuit) Diuinitatem quidem Animo, humanitatem autem exprimente Corpore. Qui quidem Diuinitatem Ducem ſecuti, cùm rectè de cognata natura ſenſerint, tùm ad virtutis normam vitam omnem direxerint, Boni ſunt omnis inter homines Auctores : qui verò mortali ac ferina parte ducti, cùm de Deo ſecus ſenſerint, tùm ad voluptatem retulerint omnia, magnorum contrà ſunt Auctores Malorum.

Inter hos Medij ſunt, & qui Gloriæ ſtudent, & qui Diuitijs : cùm ſimulacrum illa ſit virtutis, hæ voluptates concinnent.

Et in eorum quidem numero, qui virtutem ſunt amplexi, cùm alij ſæculis omnibus extitere, tum Amphitryonis F. Hercules, quem diximus bona reipubl. conſtitutione virtutiſ$\acute{q}$ ſtudio Græcis conciliato, celeberrimos illos reddidiſſe, cùm ſibi primum ipſi virtutem crebris laboribus & certaminibus comparaſſet : Lycurgus item Lacedæmonius, qui fratre Rege ſine liberis mortuo, cùm Coniunx, quæ grauidam ſe norat, ad ipſum ſe, fetu abolito, Regnum vnà cum Matrimonio delaturum recepiſſet, re non conceſſa, quoniam Iuſtitia repugnabat, fratriſ$\acute{q}$ filio tum vita conciliata, tum paterno dominio reſtituto, aliquanto pòſt tempore Legiſlator à ſuis conſtitutus, præclara illa Reip. conſtitutione introducta, celeberrimam ipſam vrbem cùm inter Græcos tùm inter Barbaros reddidit : Alexander quoque Rex Macedonum, qui per virtutem ſimul & animi magnitudinem, Græcorum Princeps effectus, ipſis pariter & Macedonibus, Aſiæ comparauit imperium:

Nec non inter Barbaros, Perſa Cyrus, qui Perſas ſuos virtute propria cùm tyrannide Medorum liberauit, tùm & borum & Aſiæ reliquæ dominos conſtituit.

K. ij.　　　　　In

In altero verò numero cùm alij recensentur, tùm Alexander Troianus, Priami filius, qui in Dearum iudicio, vitǽq́ generum electione, tùm Iunone contempta, virtutis Præside, tum Auctore gloriæ Minerua, Venerem voluptatis Deam prætulit. Quapropter neglectis tùm Regno à Iunone concesso, vita cum virtute et fœlicitate coniuncta: tùm à Minerua oblata victoria bellica, vita gloriosa: Helena verò Lacæna Tindarei F. Menelai Atridæ coniuge, præmio tam iniqui iudicij accepta, tanquam voluptatis colophone, vt corpore omnium pulcherrima, sic animo turpissima & adultera, cum hac sese simul & Patriam pessundedit. Sardanapalus item Assyrius, qui per Mollitiem et luxum, Asiæ Imperium Assyrijs quidem suis ademit, Medis autem concessit: Nec non de Romanis Nero, qui cùm alijs grauibus ac nefandis perpetratis, tùm occisa matre, seipsum quoq́ tandem malum malè perdidit. Nam
» Patriam cupiebat quidem, sed præ Romanorum virtute, nondum pote-
» rat euertere. Ac sæpè plures existunt huius generis, tùm inter Princi-
» pes, tùm inter Priuatos, alij grauius alijs peccantes :. in his etiam
» illi, qui Iustitiam quidem et Veritatem & Bonum Commune pro vm-
» bris ducunt, auro autem & similibus inhiant: fœlicitatem quidem in
» vestibus, auro, argento, luxúq́ quotidiano ponentes, Propriam verò
» simul & liberorum, et Patriæ totius Libertatem, ac SECVRITA-
» TEM negligentes. Quidam etiam donec auro & similibus, res ca-
» ret, ac per se consideratur, vehementissimè Iustitiam & Veritatem
» defendunt: Sed simul atque vel aurum, vel Auri quid simile micuerit,
» mòx & lingua ligatur, & os obturatur, ac de Iustitia quidem silent:
» Ad contraria verò, omnis illa conuertitur vehementia. Siquidem ab his
& huius generis hominibus, cum reguntur Respub. semper sunt infœlices, quando ne probissima quidem latæ legés habentur ratæ, sed omnia temerè permiscentur. Non enim tantùm probas leges requirunt Respubl. sed etiam ratas: quales quidem per virtutem Principum existunt: quam, tria præcipua Pietatis genera diximus consequi.

Postquam autem alia re nulla, quàm Salute, nunc indigemus, (non enim nos latet, quò res ex amplissimo Romanorum Imperio deuenerunt, quibus duæ tantum in Thracia relictæ sunt vrbes, et Peloponnesi pars aliqua, ac si qua restat etiam Insula,) Salutem autem Ciuitatum duntaxat è proba Republ. diximus proficisci: Respubl. nobis & legibus præstantissimis et Moderatoribus quàm fieri poterit optimis erit emendanda. Etenim quantò res nostræ peiori sunt loco, & infirmiores cum potentioribus hostibus committimur, tanto magis Rempubl. potiorem decet nos opponere, quæ reliquorum exæquet imbecillitatem.

Quibus autem rationibus optima constituatur Respub. iam diximus: pòtissimis quibúsq́ & ad rem præsentem maximè pertinentibus expo-
» sitis, ijsq́ non valdè difficilibus. Quæ enim res ex vnius voluntate effectum

Leges Ratæ

effectum suum vel sortiuntur, vel amittunt; non debent pro valdè dif- „
ficilibus haberi. Vnius porrò voluntatem, tuam potissimùm iudico. Ete- „
nim si tibi, qui Princeps noster es, & maxima polles potentia, præcla- „
ræ alicuius rei gerendæ Deus amorem inspirauerit, cùm virtutem atq; „
honestatem exactè secteris, non difficulter hæ res constitui poterunt, „
nec ampliùs erit de salute nostra desperandum. Siquidem in hòc posita „
omnia sunt, ex eoq; vel Salus nostra, vel Pernities dependet. Etenim „
si quam rem præclaram & magnam cupias gerere, nihil vel præclarius „
vel maius tùm Salute Gentis, tùm Regni SECVRITATE facilè repereris. „
Hæc autem non nisi probe Reipubl. constitutione parantur. Ea porrò
non alia ratione, quàm quæ modò fuit à nobis exposita, componitur:
quamq; omnes vbiq; laudatæ sunt Ciuitates secutæ. Ac si duntaxat ip- „
se volueris, & hoc fueris animo, nullo negocio socios operis inuenies: „
probiores quidem primos muneribus destinans, reliquos autem benefa-
ctis & mulctis corrigens: ac duobus his, tùm cupiditate bonorum, tùm
contra peccantes ira ritè vsus. Siquidem nec absentia bona cuiquam li- „
cet adipisci, nisi cum labore desideret: nec præsentia seruare, nisi ra- „
tioni ira obtemperet.

Ac Reipubl. Constitutionem, si videtur, à Consultoribus ordire: e- • Consultores
osq; tibi cùm alijs, tùm numero instructissimos, quemadmodum præce-
pimus, constitue. Siquidem hinc æquum est incipere: cumq; maiori par-
ti visum quid fuerit, ita demùm rerum mutationē & emendationem ag-
gredi. Neq; illos lateat, quanto res nostræ versentur in discrimine,
quantumq; salutis indigi simus: nec eam nisi emendata Republ. possi-
mus consequi. Nam & qui ægrotant, si consueta viuendi ratione læ-
duntur, non aliter sanantur, quàm cum hac omissa, commodiorem deli-
gunt.

Deindè, maiorem exercitus partem expurga: diuisis bifariam Pelo-
ponnesijs: in Militantes, & Collationem pendentes, prout singulorum
feret ratio: sic, vt non ampliùs ijdē simul et Militent et pendant. Etenim
nec teipsum pariter et gentem seruare poteris, nisi hostes deuiceris: nec
hostes deuincere, nisi exercitum potiùs beneuolum & animosum, quàm „
copiosum habueris. Difficulter autem, pendens Exercitus, beneuolen- „
tiam simul & animos conseruat: sed vtrumq; ferè, perdit.

Præfecti quoq; secernantur à Mercatoribus: & cunctis quidem im- Præfecti
peretur, ne Mercaturam vel Institoriam deinceps exerceant: sed se pro
Præfectis gerant, Reipubl. custodiam et salutem procurantes, non ser-
uilia obeuntes officia, & quidem nequam seruorum, qui ponderibus
iniustis & quacunq; re alia miseros Rusticos damno afficiunt. Sin e-
tiam de Mercatoribus aliqui fuerint ad Magistratus euecti, ij vel re-
licta Mercatura, si fuerint idonei, munere fungantur: vel loco moue-
antur. Oportet enim hæc secerni, non Præfectos cum Mercatoribus per-
misceri, nec Milites agros colere, nec Rusticis communem salutem com-

K. iij.   mitti

mitti: quæ funt omnia Reipubl. prauiſſimæ, quaq́ nihil vnquam magnum vel præclarum geſſerit. Enimuero nec Aſinis ad Equorum vtimur opera, nec Equis ad Aſinorum: adeoq́ nec Equis yſdem ad omnia, verùm alijs bello, alijs ad ſarcinas. At hoc diſcrimen, in hominibus multo magis obſeruandum erat. Tributis quoq; multis iſtis, crebris, & inæqualibus ſublatis, illud omnium loco repone, quod rerum
naſcentium Tertiam diximus æquiſſimè complecti partem, leuiſſimum
pendentibus & Reipublicæ vtiliſſimum idem futurum. Nam propter
hoc Tributum, nec temerè quis aufugiet, nec ab exactoribus iniuriam
accipiet, dum illi pendentibus quamplurima volunt attribuere, quo videlicet ſimul Tributum creſcat. De his autem Hilotis, primùm tuæ
familiæ, quot videbitur opus, ſelige: reliquos deinde Præfectis et Militibus primarys, quanto voles numero concede. Tum verò cogantur
ſinguli pro Hilotarum aſcriptorum numero Clientes alere, ſeruos vide-
» licet militares: ne pecuniam publicam temerè profundant: quæq́ hoſtes
» in votis habent, vt Salutis Communis impenſæ turpiter diſſipentur, ip-
» ſi videantur procurare.   *   *   *

*   *   *   *   *   *

Hæc quoq́ Naturæ conſideres licet Exempla. § Aquila Rex quidem eſt
Auium, & Ioui fuit olim conſecratus, minimè tamen varias aut ful-
gentes habet Alas. Pauo contrà varius quidem eſt & fulgens, ſed minimè Regia natura. Pluresq́ Aues aliæ Pauone longè viliores, colo-
rum ſunt varietate diſtinctæ. Quare videtur, qui veſtibus prætextis
àc ſimilibus * ſuperbit, tanquam Pauonis pulcritudine gloriari. Iam illud ſpecta, ſitne honeſtius ac iucundius, huc præcipuè tendentem, &
bello quantùm licet conſulentem, moderato tùm veſtitu, tùm reliquo
viuendi modo, hoſtes quídem contemnere, de Imperio autem ac Regno
Securum eſſe: an veſte prætexta inuolutum, tremere, et hoſtes metu-
ere. Quòd ſi porrò Paſtores eſſetis, vtro modo lac impenderetis? Vtrùm
partem quidem alteram ipſi conſumeretis, altera verò canes robuſtos a-
leretis, qui à ferarum inſidys Ouile defenderent: vt eo conſeruato tùm
Paſtores eſſe, tum fructibus diù frui poſſetis: an hoc neglecto, partem
quidem alteram ingurgitaretis & veſtimenta prolueretis, altera verò,
Canum robuſtorum loco, Maliteos catellos & vulpes aleretis, aut Vr-
ſos, vt voraciſſimas Beſtias, ita parùm intentas cuſtodiæ?   *

*   *   *   *   *   *

Huc igitur omne ſtudium conuerte, nihil omittens neq; prætexens,
ſiue quid aut priorum Regum alicui, aut ipſi tibi aliter olim fuit viſum, ſiue quibuſdam non eſt res placitura: ſed cùm omnia mouens,
tùm nihil non ad Communem ſalutem pertinere viſum tentans, quando
ne Medici quidem ſua ſemper poſſunt ſeruare decreta, ſed cum omnia
mouent, tum nihil ad ſanitatem pertinens omittunt, ac ſecant etiam,
vel vrunt, manumq́ interdum vel Pedem inſuper ob ſalutem totius corporis

poris abſcindunt. Horum ſiquidem ipſe quædam, ſi videbitur, cum li-
ceat, perages: nonnulla ab Auguſto Imperatore, & Patre, Salutis
Publicæ cauſa poſtulabis. Neque tibi ille difficulter ea concedet, cùm
huc ſpectare cognouerit, Ingenium ſimul & Impetum diuinum admi-
ratus. Cæterum his, quæ maximè & proximè videntur ad Salutem
tendere peractis, reliqua ſine vlla difficultate deinceps, quæcunq; ad
Reipubl. virtutem & ornatum pertinent, aſſequeris: ac tandem op-
timam omnino Rempubl. nobis conſtitues. Quanto quidem maior
tibi à nobis habetur honor, tantò etiam iacturam fore
credes maiorem, ſi quid ſecus euenerit. Enimuerò te
potiſsimùm Salutis Communis decet curam gerere,
nihil Cunctantem, nec differentem. Siquidem
nec licèt cunctari, cùm ſit præ foribus
periculum: nec alioqui tale negoti-
um conuenit differre. Nec
imperitè videtur He-
ſiodus dicere:

SEMPER AT IGNAVVS CVM NOXIS PRÆLIA MISCIT.

AND with this pithy peece of wiſe warning, by HESIODVS (very
aptly to our preſent purpoſe) recorded, I will end this firſt Treatiſe:
falling out, in very good Oportunitie, to be in ſtead of a Preface,
for the better vnderſtanding and enioying the reſt of the RARE MEMO-
RIALS enſuing: collected, according to the Title prefixed. For which
Preface, being thus, (though with more zeale than cunning) finiſhed, I
yeld thanks moſt humbly to the Omnipotent Spirit of Veritie, the Spirit
of all Comfort and Bountifulnes: which Directed & enclined the Minde
and Tongue of my Inſtructer, thus to prefer the SAFETY AND POLI-
TIKELY ASSVRED PEACE VNIVERSALL, OF THIS BRYTISH KING-
DOM, before any other Lucre, or Honor, Publike or Priuate: As, without which PEACE AND TRANQVILLITY, neither the COMMONS: nor,
the LORDES SPIRITVALL OR TEMPORALL: no, nor yet our moſt
GRACIOVS ELIZABETH, can atteyne to the excellent Scope, and perfection of Ciuill State: vnto which, both, by the Law of God and Nature: and alſo by Humaine Policy, all ſound Common-Wealths, and
Bodies Politike, ought to direct all their Actions Ciuill.

And I beſeche you (Right Worſhipfull Sir,) not onely to take theſe my
ſpeedy Trauailes and Collections in good parte, your ſelfe: But alſo, to
whom ſo euer, you will deliuer any one of the Copies, (wherof, only one
Hundred are to be printed, by the warning of my Inſtructor:) You would
be my Carefull Orator, to this purpoſe chiefly: That my good will, and
exceding zealous Intent herein, dutifully to pleaſure this BRYTISH MO-
NARCHIE, might be thankfully accepted: and ſo, my ſimple & very faythfull Trauailes, to be rewarded. And finally, that you would very earneſt-

*Hæc, magnorum hominum sunt: Hæc, apud Maiores nostros factitata: Hæc genera Officiorum qui persequuntur, cum summa Vtilitate Reipublicæ, magnam ipsi adipiscuntur & Gratiam & Gloriam. Cicero, Offic. lib. 2.

ly request * them, (for the Common-Wealths Cavse,). Speedily, Circumspectly, and Paradoxally to vewe this plat. And then, to amend the Imperfection: and to Supply the wants thereof: (the better now to be espied, by these few warnings,) and prosperously, to farder some pithy Extract made of the whole matter: So much, as they, both by their Politike skill, and auailable Authority, best can: And, Then, shall the foresaid Psalmody, most aptly and hartily, of all true Brytish And English Svbiects, be song:

> Lauda HIERVSALEM Dominum,
>   Lauda Deam tuum SION.
> Quoniam confortauit Seras Portarum tuarum:
>   Benedixit filijs tuis in te.
> Qui posuit fines tuos PACEM,
>   Et adipe Frumenti satiat te. &c.
> Non fecit Taliter omni Nationi.

Prayse we all the Lord therfore.
Amen.

Finished, Anno Domini. 1576.
Augusto Mense.

Printed At London By Iohn
Daye, Anno 1577.
In Septemb.

Cum Priuilegio Regiæ Maiestatis.

TO THE RIGHT WORSHIPFVL M. CHRISTOPHER
Hatton , Efquyer , Capitayn of her Maiefties
Garde , and Ientleman of her Priuy Chamber .

YF Priuat wealth, be leef and deere,
To any VVight, of Brytifh Soyl:
Ought Publik Weale , haue any peere ?
To that, is due, all Wealth and Toyl.

Anno:
1576. Wherof, fuch Lore as I (of * late,)
Haue lernd, and for Security,
By Godly means, to Garde this State,
To you I fend, now, carefully.

Unto the Gardians, moft wife,
And Sacred Senat, or Chief Powr,
I durft not offer this Aduife,
(So homely writ,) for fear of Lowr.

But, at your will, and difcreet choyce,
To keep by you, or to imparte,
I leaue this zealous Publik voyce:
You will accept fo fimple parte.

M'Inftructors freend did warrant me,
You would fo do, as he did his:
E.D.
Efq. That * Redy freend, can witnes be,
For Higher States, what written is:

Of Gratefulnes, due Argument.
Yf greeuous wound , of fklandrous Darte,
At length to cure, they will be bent,
M'Inftructor, then, will doo his parte,

In erneft wife, I know right well:
No Merit fhall forgotten ly.
Thus much , I thought, was good to tell:
God graunt you Blis, aboue the Sky.